MznLnx

Missing Links Exam Preps

Exam Prep for

Operations Management

Gaither & Frazier, 9th Edition

The MznLnx Exam Prep is your link from the texbook and lecture to your exams.
The MznLnx Exam Preps are unauthorized and comprehensive reviews of your textbooks.

All material provided by MznLnx and Rico Publications (c) 2010
Textbook publishers and textbook authors do not particpate in or contribute to these reviews.

MznLnx

Rico
Publications

Exam Prep for Operations Management
9th Edition
Gaither & Frazier

Publisher: Raymond Houge
Assistant Editor: Michael Rouger
Text and Cover Designer: Lisa Buckner
Marketing Manager: Sara Swagger
Project Manager, Editorial Production: Jerry Emerson
Art Director: Vernon Lowerui

Product Manager: Dave Mason
Editorial Assitant: Rachel Guzmanji
Pedagogy: Debra Long
Cover Image: Jim Reed/Getty Images
Text and Cover Printer: City Printing, Inc.
Compositor: Media Mix, Inc.

(c) 2010 Rico Publications
ALL RIGHTS RESERVED. No part of this work covered by the copyright may be reproduced or used in any form or by an means--graphic, electronic, or mechanical, including photocopying, recording, taping, Web distribution, information storage, and retrieval systems, or in any other manner--without the written permission of the publisher.

Printed in the United States
ISBN:

For more information about our products, contact us at:
Dave.Mason@RicoPublications.com

For permission to use material from this text or product, submit a request online to:
Dave.Mason@RicoPublications.com

Contents

CHAPTER 1
Introduction to Operations Management — 1

CHAPTER 2
Operations Strategies in a Global Economy — 7

CHAPTER 3
Demand Forecasting — 14

CHAPTER 4
Product, Process, and Service Design — 25

CHAPTER 5
Facility Capacity, Location, and Layout — 35

CHAPTER 6
Operations Technologies — 43

CHAPTER 7
Operations Quality Management — 51

CHAPTER 8
Strategic Allocation of Resources — 61

CHAPTER 9
Service Operations Planning and Scheduling — 64

CHAPTER 10
Project Management — 66

CHAPTER 11
Supply Chain Management and E-Business — 71

CHAPTER 12
Just-in-Time and Lean Manufacturing — 79

CHAPTER 13
Production Planning — 84

CHAPTER 14
Inventory Management — 90

CHAPTER 15
Resource Requirements Planning: MRP and CRP — 97

CHAPTER 16
Manufacturing Operations Scheduling — 100

CHAPTER 17
Quality Control — 103

CHAPTER 18
Employee Productivity — 109

CHAPTER 19
Maintenance Management — 113

ANSWER KEY — 118

TO THE STUDENT

COMPREHENSIVE

The *MznLnx* Exam Prep series is designed to help you pass your exams. Editors at MznLnx review your textbooks and then prepare these practice exams to help you master the textbook material. Unlike study guides, workbooks, and practice tests provided by the texbook publisher and textbook authors, *MznLnx* gives you **all** of the material in each chapter in exam form, not just samples, so you can be sure to nail your exam.

MECHANICAL

The MznLnx Exam Prep series creates exams that will help you learn the subject matter as well as test you on your understanding. Each question is designed to help you master the concept. Just working through the exams, you gain an understanding of the subject--its a simple mechanical process that produces success.

INTEGRATED STUDY GUIDE AND REVIEW

MznLnx is not just a set of exams designed to test you, its also a comprehensive review of the subject content. Each exam question is also a review of the concept, making sure that you will get the answer correct without having to go to other sources of material. You learn as you go! Its the easiest way to pass an exam.

HUMOR

Studying can be tedious and dry. MznLnx's instructional design includes moderate humor within the exam questions on occassion, to break the tedium and revitalize the brain

Chapter 1. Introduction to Operations Management 1

1. _____ is an area of business concerned with the production of goods and services, and involves the responsibility of ensuring that business operations are efficient in terms of using as little resource as needed, and effective in terms of meeting customer requirements. It is concerned with managing the process that converts inputs (in the forms of materials, labour and energy) into outputs (in the form of goods and services.)

Operations traditionally refers to the production of goods and services separately, although the distinction between these two main types of operations is increasingly difficult to make as manufacturers tend to merge product and service offerings.

   a. AAAI
   b. A Stake in the Outcome
   c. Operations management
   d. A4e

2. A _____ is a computer program typically used to provide some form of artificial intelligence, which consists primarily of a set of rules about behavior. These rules, termed productions, are a basic representation found useful in AI planning, expert systems and action selection. A _____ provides the mechanism necessary to execute productions in order to achieve some goal for the system.
   a. 33 Strategies of War
   b. Production system
   c. 28-hour day
   d. 1990 Clean Air Act

3. The _____ was a period in the late 18th and early 19th centuries when major changes in agriculture, manufacturing, mining, and transportation had a profound effect on the socioeconomic and cultural conditions in Britain. The changes subsequently spread throughout Europe, North America, and eventually the world. The onset of the _____ marked a major turning point in human society; almost every aspect of daily life was eventually influenced in some way.
   a. Abraham Harold Maslow
   b. Adam Smith
   c. Affiliation
   d. Industrial revolution

4. _____ are parts that are for practical purposes identical. They are made to specifications that ensure that they are so nearly identical that they will fit into any device of the same type. One such part can freely replace another, without any custom fitting (such as filing.)
   a. AAAI
   b. A Stake in the Outcome
   c. Interchangeable parts
   d. A4e

Chapter 1. Introduction to Operations Management

5. _____ was a Scottish moral philosopher and a pioneer of political economy. One of the key figures of the Scottish Enlightenment, Smith is the author of The Theory of Moral Sentiments and An Inquiry into the Nature and Causes of the Wealth of Nations. The latter, usually abbreviated as The Wealth of Nations, is considered his magnum opus and the first modern work of economics.
   a. Affiliation
   b. Affirmative action
   c. Abraham Harold Maslow
   d. Adam Smith

6. _____ is a theory of management that analyzes and synthesizes workflows, with the objective of improving labour productivity. The core ideas of the theory were developed by Frederick Winslow Taylor in the 1880s and 1890s, and were first published in his monographs, Shop Management and The Principles of _____ Taylor believed that decisions based upon tradition and rules of thumb should be replaced by precise procedures developed after careful study of an individual at work.
   a. Value engineering
   b. Capacity planning
   c. Master production schedule
   d. Scientific management

7. _____, widely known as F. W. Taylor, was an American mechanical engineer who sought to improve industrial efficiency. He is regarded as the father of scientific management, and was one of the first management consultants.

Taylor was one of the intellectual leaders of the Efficiency Movement and his ideas, broadly conceived, were highly influential in the Progressive Era.

   a. Geoffrey Colvin
   b. Douglas N. Daft
   c. Jonah Jacob Goldberg
   d. Frederick Winslow Taylor

8. Industrial engineering is also known as operations management, management science, systems engineering, or manufacturing engineering; a distinction that seems to depend on the viewpoint or motives of the user. Recruiters or educational establishments use the names to differentiate themselves from others. In healthcare, for example, _____ are more commonly known as management engineers or health systems engineers.
   a. A4e
   b. A Stake in the Outcome
   c. Industrial engineers
   d. AAAI

Chapter 1. Introduction to Operations Management

9. _____ was a writer, management consultant, and self-described 'social ecologist.' Widely considered to be 'the father of modern management,' his 39 books and countless scholarly and popular articles explored how humans are organized across all sectors of society--in business, government and the nonprofit world. His writings have predicted many of the major developments of the late twentieth century, including privatization and decentralization; the rise of Japan to economic world power; the decisive importance of marketing; and the emergence of the information society with its necessity of lifelong learning. In 1959, Drucker coined the term 'knowledge worker' and later in his life considered knowledge work productivity to be the next frontier of management.
   a. Debora L. Spar
   b. Jacques Al-Salawat Nasruddin Nasser
   c. Chrissie Hynde
   d. Peter Ferdinand Drucker

10. _____ Movement refers to those researchers of organizational development who study the behavior of people in groups, in particular workplace groups. It originated in the 1920s' Hawthorne studies, which examined the effects of social relations, motivation and employee satisfaction on factory productivity. The movement viewed workers in terms of their psychology and fit with companies, rather than as interchangeable parts.
    a. Participatory management
    b. Hersey-Blanchard situational theory
    c. Human relations
    d. Work design

11. _____ refers to those researchers of organizational development who study the behavior of people in groups, in particular workplace groups. It originated in the 1920s' Hawthorne studies, which examined the effects of social relations, motivation and employee satisfaction on factory productivity. The movement viewed workers in terms of their psychology and fit with companies, rather than as interchangeable parts.
    a. Job analysis
    b. Job satisfaction
    c. Path-goal theory
    d. Human relations movement

12. _____ is the production of large amounts of standardized products, including and especially on assembly lines. The concepts of _____ are applied to various kinds of products, from fluids and particulates handled in bulk to discrete solid parts to assemblies of such parts

_____ of assemblies typically uses electric-motor-powered moving tracks or conveyor belts to move partially complete products to workers, who perform simple repetitive tasks.

Chapter 1. Introduction to Operations Management

   a. 1990 Clean Air Act
   b. 33 Strategies of War
   c. 28-hour day
   d. Mass production

13. _____ in the USA, Canada, South Africa and Australia, and operational research in Europe, is an interdisciplinary branch of applied mathematics and formal science that uses methods such as mathematical modeling, statistics, and algorithms to arrive at optimal or near optimal solutions to complex problems. It is typically concerned with optimizing the maxima (profit, assembly line performance, crop yield, bandwidth, etc) or minima (loss, risk, etc.) of some objective function.

   a. AAAI
   b. A Stake in the Outcome
   c. A4e
   d. Operations research

14. _____ is an advertisement in which a particular product specifically mentions a competitor by name for the express purpose of showing why the competitor is inferior to the product naming it.

This should not be confused with parody advertisements, where a fictional product is being advertised for the purpose of poking fun at the particular advertisement, nor should it be confused with the use of a coined brand name for the purpose of comparing the product without actually naming an actual competitor. ('Wikipedia tastes better and is less filling than the Encyclopedia Galactica.')

In the 1980s, during what has been referred to as the cola wars, soft-drink manufacturer Pepsi ran a series of advertisements where people, caught on hidden camera, in a blind taste test, chose Pepsi over rival Coca-Cola.

   a. 28-hour day
   b. 33 Strategies of War
   c. 1990 Clean Air Act
   d. Comparative advertising

15. _____ is a company-wide computer software system used to manage and coordinate all the resources, information, and functions of a business from shared data stores.

An _____ system has a service-oriented architecture with modular hardware and software units and 'services' that communicate on a local area network. The modular design allows a business to add or reconfigure modules (perhaps from different vendors) while preserving data integrity in one shared database that may be centralized or distributed.

a. AAAI
b. Enterprise resource planning
c. A Stake in the Outcome
d. A4e

16. _____ can be regarded as an outcome of mental processes (cognitive process) leading to the selection of a course of action among several alternatives. Every _____ process produces a final choice. The output can be an action or an opinion of choice.
    a. 28-hour day
    b. 33 Strategies of War
    c. 1990 Clean Air Act
    d. Decision making

17. _____ is one of the managerial functions like planning, organizing, staffing and directing. It is an important function because it helps to check the errors and to take the corrective action so that deviation from standards are minimized and stated goals of the organization are achieved in desired manner. According to modern concepts, _____ is a foreseeing action whereas earlier concept of _____ was used only when errors were detected. _____ in management means setting standards, measuring actual performance and taking corrective action.
    a. Turnover
    b. Decision tree pruning
    c. Schedule of reinforcement
    d. Control

18. A _____ is a list of the general tasks and responsibilities of a position. Typically, it also includes to whom the position reports, specifications such as the qualifications needed by the person in the job, salary range for the position, etc. A _____ is usually developed by conducting a job analysis, which includes examining the tasks and sequences of tasks necessary to perform the job.
    a. Recruitment Process Insourcing
    b. Job description
    c. Recruitment advertising
    d. Recruitment

19. In economics, a _____ is a function that specifies the output of a firm, an industry, or an entire economy for all combinations of inputs. A meta-_____ compares the practice of the existing entities converting inputs X into output y to determine the most efficient practice _____ of the existing entities, whether the most efficient feasible practice production or the most efficient actual practice production. In either case, the maximum output of a technologically-determined production process is a mathematical function of input factors of production.

a. Multifactor productivity
b. Factors of production
c. Production function
d. Diseconomies of scale

Chapter 2. Operations Strategies in a Global Economy

1. _____ is an advertisement in which a particular product specifically mentions a competitor by name for the express purpose of showing why the competitor is inferior to the product naming it.

This should not be confused with parody advertisements, where a fictional product is being advertised for the purpose of poking fun at the particular advertisement, nor should it be confused with the use of a coined brand name for the purpose of comparing the product without actually naming an actual competitor. ('Wikipedia tastes better and is less filling than the Encyclopedia Galactica.')

In the 1980s, during what has been referred to as the cola wars, soft-drink manufacturer Pepsi ran a series of advertisements where people, caught on hidden camera, in a blind taste test, chose Pepsi over rival Coca-Cola.

  a. 28-hour day
  b. Comparative advertising
  c. 33 Strategies of War
  d. 1990 Clean Air Act

2. _____ is a type of trade policy that allows traders to act and transact without interference from government. Thus, the policy permits trading partners mutual gains from trade, with goods and services produced according to the theory of comparative advantage.

Under a _____ policy, prices are a reflection of true supply and demand, and are the sole determinant of resource allocation.

  a. Free Trade
  b. 1990 Clean Air Act
  c. 33 Strategies of War
  d. 28-hour day

3. _____ is a designated group of countries that have agreed to eliminate tariffs, quotas and preferences on most (if not all) goods and services traded between them. It can be considered the second stage of economic integration. Countries choose this kind of economic integration form if their economical structures are complementary.
  a. 1990 Clean Air Act
  b. 33 Strategies of War
  c. Free trade area
  d. 28-hour day

4. The _____ is a trilateral trade bloc in North America created by the governments of the United States, Canada, and Mexico. The agreement creating the trade bloc came into force on January 1, 1994. It superseded the Canada-United States Free Trade Agreement between the U.S. and Canada.

Chapter 2. Operations Strategies in a Global Economy

   a. Business war game
   b. Trade union
   c. Career portfolios
   d. North American Free Trade Agreement

5. The _____ is an international organization designed by its founders to supervise and liberalize international trade. The organization officially commenced on 1 January 1995, under the Marrakesh Agreement, succeeding the 1947 General Agreement on Tariffs and Trade (GATT.)

The _____ deals with regulation of trade between participating countries; it provides a framework for negotiating and formalising trade agreements, and a dispute resolution process aimed at enforcing participants' adherence to _____ agreements which are signed by representatives of member governments and ratified by their parliaments.

   a. 1990 Clean Air Act
   b. Network planning and design
   c. World Trade Organization
   d. National Institute for Occupational Safety and Health

6. _____ was a writer, management consultant, and self-described 'social ecologist.' Widely considered to be 'the father of modern management,' his 39 books and countless scholarly and popular articles explored how humans are organized across all sectors of society--in business, government and the nonprofit world. His writings have predicted many of the major developments of the late twentieth century, including privatization and decentralization; the rise of Japan to economic world power; the decisive importance of marketing; and the emergence of the information society with its necessity of lifelong learning. In 1959, Drucker coined the term 'knowledge worker' and later in his life considered knowledge work productivity to be the next frontier of management.
   a. Chrissie Hynde
   b. Debora L. Spar
   c. Jacques Al-Salawat Nasruddin Nasser
   d. Peter Ferdinand Drucker

7. A _____ is a set of companies with interlocking business relationships and shareholdings. It is a type of business group.

The prototypical _____ are those which appeared in Japan during the 'economic miracle' following World War II.

Chapter 2. Operations Strategies in a Global Economy

a. 33 Strategies of War
b. 28-hour day
c. 1990 Clean Air Act
d. Keiretsu

8. A _____ is a formal relationship between two or more parties to pursue a set of agreed upon goals or to meet a critical business need while remaining independent organizations.

Partners may provide the _____ with resources such as products, distribution channels, manufacturing capability, project funding, capital equipment, knowledge, expertise, or intellectual property. The alliance is a cooperation or collaboration which aims for a synergy where each partner hopes that the benefits from the alliance will be greater than those from individual efforts.

a. Process automation
b. Strategic alliance
c. Golden parachute
d. Farmshoring

9. _____ in its literal sense is the process of transformation of local or regional phenomena into global ones. It can be described as a process by which the people of the world are unified into a single society and function together.

This process is a combination of economic, technological, sociocultural and political forces.

a. Histogram
b. Globalization
c. Collaborative Planning, Forecasting and Replenishment
d. Cost Management

10. In economics, business, retail, and accounting, a _____ is the value of money that has been used up to produce something, and hence is not available for use anymore. In economics, a _____ is an alternative that is given up as a result of a decision. In business, the _____ may be one of acquisition, in which case the amount of money expended to acquire it is counted as _____.

a. Fixed costs
b. Cost overrun
c. Cost allocation
d. Cost

11. _____ is the provision of service to customers before, during and after a purchase.

According to Turban et al. (2002), '_____ is a series of activities designed to enhance the level of customer satisfaction - that is, the feeling that a product or service has met the customer expectation.'

Its importance varies by product, industry and customer; defective or broken merchandise can be exchanged, often only with a receipt and within a specified time frame.

   a. Customer service
   b. Service rate
   c. 28-hour day
   d. 1990 Clean Air Act

12. _____ is a company-wide computer software system used to manage and coordinate all the resources, information, and functions of a business from shared data stores.

An _____ system has a service-oriented architecture with modular hardware and software units and 'services' that communicate on a local area network. The modular design allows a business to add or reconfigure modules (perhaps from different vendors) while preserving data integrity in one shared database that may be centralized or distributed.

   a. A4e
   b. AAAI
   c. Enterprise resource planning
   d. A Stake in the Outcome

13. Labor intensity is the relative proportion of labor (compared to capital) used in a process. The term '_____' can be used when proposing the amount of work that is assigned to each worker/employee (labor), emphasizing on the skill involved in the respective line of work.
   a. Labor intensive
   b. Cost-effectiveness
   c. Private placement
   d. Choquet integral

14. A _____ is a relatively new executive level position at a corporation, company, organization typically reporting directly to the CEO or board of directors. The _____ is responsible for a brand's image, experience, and promise, and propagating it throughout all aspects of the company. The brand officer oversees marketing, advertising, design, public relations and customer service departments.

Chapter 2. Operations Strategies in a Global Economy

a. Director of communications
b. Chief executive officer
c. Purchasing manager
d. Chief brand officer

15. The _____ is a piece of United States environmental policy relating to the reduction of smog and air pollution. It follows the Clean Air Act in 1963, the Clean Air Act Amendment in 1966, the Clean Air Act Extension in 1970, and the Clean Air Act Amendments in 1977. It was enacted by the 101st United States Congress (Pub.L.
 a. Robinson-Patman Act
 b. 1990 Clean Air Act
 c. Family and Medical Leave Act of 1993
 d. Reverification

16. _____ is a broad label that refers to any individuals or households that use goods and services generated within the economy. The concept of a _____ is used in different contexts, so that the usage and significance of the term may vary.

Typically when business people and economists talk of _____s they are talking about person as _____, an aggregated commodity item with little individuality other than that expressed in the buy/not-buy decision.

 a. 1990 Clean Air Act
 b. 28-hour day
 c. 33 Strategies of War
 d. Consumer

17. The _____, widely known as ISO , is an international-standard-setting body composed of representatives from various national standards organizations. Founded on 23 February 1947, the organization promulgates worldwide proprietary industrial and commercial standards. It is headquartered in Geneva, Switzerland.
 a. A4e
 b. AAAI
 c. A Stake in the Outcome
 d. International Organization for Standardization

18. _____ refers to the aggregated strategies of single business firm or a strategic business unit (SBU) in a diversified corporation. According to Michael Porter, a firm must formulate a _____ that incorporates either cost leadership, differentiation or focus in order to achieve a sustainable competitive advantage and long-term success in its chosen arenas or industries.

Functional strategies include marketing strategies, new product development strategies, human resource strategies, financial strategies, legal strategies, supply-chain strategies, and information technology management strategies.

   a. Strategic thinking
   b. Switching cost
   c. Competitive heterogeneity
   d. Business strategy

19. A _____ is a computer program typically used to provide some form of artificial intelligence, which consists primarily of a set of rules about behavior. These rules, termed productions, are a basic representation found useful in AI planning, expert systems and action selection. A _____ provides the mechanism necessary to execute productions in order to achieve some goal for the system.
   a. 1990 Clean Air Act
   b. Production system
   c. 28-hour day
   d. 33 Strategies of War

20. In marketing, _____ has come to mean the process by which marketers try to create an image or identity in the minds of their target market for its product, brand, or organization. It is the 'relative competitive comparison' their product occupies in a given market as perceived by the target market.

Re-_____ involves changing the identity of a product, relative to the identity of competing products, in the collective minds of the target market.

   a. PEST analysis
   b. Context analysis
   c. Customer analytics
   d. Positioning

21. In economics, _____ is the desire to own something and the ability to pay for it. The term _____ signifies the ability or the willingness to buy a particular commodity at a given point of time.
   a. Demand
   b. 1990 Clean Air Act
   c. 33 Strategies of War
   d. 28-hour day

22. _____ is subcontracting a process, such as product design or manufacturing, to a third-party company. The decision to outsource is often made in the interest of lowering cost or making better use of time and energy costs, redirecting or conserving energy directed at the competencies of a particular business, or to make more efficient use of land, labor, capital, (information) technology and resources. _____ became part of the business lexicon during the 1980s.
   a. Unemployment insurance
   b. Opinion leadership
   c. Operant conditioning
   d. Outsourcing

23. _____ Management is the succession of strategies used by management as a product goes through its _____. The conditions in which a product is sold changes over time and must be managed as it moves through its succession of stages.

The _____ goes through many phases, involves many professional disciplines, and requires many skills, tools and processes.

   a. Product life cycle
   b. Job hunting
   c. Strategic Alliance
   d. Golden handshake

24. _____ is an integrated communications-based process through which individuals and communities discover that existing and newly-identified needs and wants may be satisfied by the products and services of others.

_____ is defined by the American _____ Association as the activity, set of institutions, and processes for creating, communicating, delivering, and exchanging offerings that have value for customers, clients, partners, and society at large. The term developed from the original meaning which referred literally to going to market, as in shopping, or going to a market to buy or sell goods or services.

   a. Market development
   b. Marketing
   c. Customer relationship management
   d. Disruptive technology

Chapter 3. Demand Forecasting

1. _____ is the process of estimation in unknown situations. Prediction is a similar, but more general term. Both can refer to estimation of time series, cross-sectional or longitudinal data.
    a. 1990 Clean Air Act
    b. 33 Strategies of War
    c. 28-hour day
    d. Forecasting

2. _____ is an area of business concerned with the production of goods and services, and involves the responsibility of ensuring that business operations are efficient in terms of using as little resource as needed, and effective in terms of meeting customer requirements. It is concerned with managing the process that converts inputs (in the forms of materials, labour and energy) into outputs (in the form of goods and services.)

Operations traditionally refers to the production of goods and services separately, although the distinction between these two main types of operations is increasingly difficult to make as manufacturers tend to merge product and service offerings.

   a. A4e
   b. AAAI
   c. Operations management
   d. A Stake in the Outcome

3. The _____ is a systematic, interactive forecasting method which relies on a panel of independent experts. The carefully selected experts answer questionnaires in two or more rounds. After each round, a facilitator provides an anonymous summary of the experts' forecasts from the previous round as well as the reasons they provided for their judgments.
    a. Delphi method
    b. Quality function deployment
    c. Hoshin Kanri
    d. Learning organization

4. In statistics, signal processing, and many other fields, a _____ is a sequence of data points, measured typically at successive times, spaced at (often uniform) time intervals. _____ analysis comprises methods that attempt to understand such _____, often either to understand the underlying context of the data points (Where did they come from? What generated them?), or to make forecasts (predictions.) _____ forecasting is the use of a model to forecast future events based on known past events: to forecast future data points before they are measured.
    a. Histogram
    b. Moving average
    c. Standard deviation
    d. Time series

Chapter 3. Demand Forecasting 15

5. In the fields of science, engineering, industry and statistics, _____ is the degree of closeness of a measured or calculated quantity to its actual (true) value. _____ is closely related to precision, also called reproducibility or repeatability, the degree to which further measurements or calculations show the same or similar results. _____ indicates proximity to the true value, precision to the repeatability or reproducibility of the measurement

The results of calculations or a measurement can be accurate but not precise, precise but not accurate, neither, or both.

   a. A4e
   b. AAAI
   c. A Stake in the Outcome
   d. Accuracy

6. _____ of the learning curve effect and the closely related experience curve effect express the relationship between equations for experience and efficiency or between efficiency gains and investment in the effort. The experience of 'learning curves' was first observed by the 19th Century German psychologist Hermann Ebbinghaus according to the difficulty of memorizing varying numbers of verbal stimuli, and subsequent learning about the complex processes of learning are discussed in the

.

The rule used for representing the learning curve effect states that the more times a task has been performed, the less time will be required on each subsequent iteration.

   a. Point biserial correlation coefficient
   b. Models
   c. Spatial Decision Support Systems
   d. Distribution

7. In statistics, a _____ is the difference between the actual or real and the predicted or forecast value of a time series or any other phenomenon of interest.

In simple cases, a forecast is compared with an outcome at a single time-point and a summary of _____ s is constructed over a collection of such time-points. Here the forecast may be assessed using the difference or using a proportional error.

a. 33 Strategies of War
b. Forecast error
c. 1990 Clean Air Act
d. 28-hour day

8. In statistics, many time series exhibit cyclic variation known as _____, periodic variation, or periodic fluctuations. This variation can be either regular or semiregular.

For example, retail sales tend to peak for the Christmas season and then decline after the holidays.

a. 1990 Clean Air Act
b. 28-hour day
c. 33 Strategies of War
d. Seasonality

9. The term '_____' refers to the concept of collecting information and attempting to spot a pattern in the information. In some fields of study, the term '_____' has more formally-defined meanings.

In project management _____ is a mathematical technique that uses historical results to predict future outcome.

a. Trend analysis
b. Stepwise regression
c. Least squares
d. Regression analysis

10. In statistics, _____ is used for two things:

- to construct a simple formula that will predict a value or values for a variable given the value of another variable.
- to test whether and how a given variable is related to another variable or variables.

_____ is a form of regression analysis in which the relationship between one or more independent variables and another variable, called the dependent variable, is modelled by a least squares function, called a _____ equation. This function is a linear combination of one or more model parameters, called regression coefficients. A _____ equation with one independent variable represents a straight line when the predicted value (i.e. the dependent variable from the regression equation) is plotted against the independent variable: this is called a simple _____. However, note that 'linear' does not refer to this straight line, but rather to the way in which the regression coefficients occur in the regression equation.

a. Clinical decision support systems
b. Continuous
c. Strict liability
d. Linear regression

11. In statistics, _____ indicates the strength and direction of a linear relationship between two random variables. That is in contrast with the usage of the term in colloquial speech, which denotes any relationship, not necessarily linear. In general statistical usage, _____ or co-relation refers to the departure of two random variables from independence.
   a. Heteroskedastic
   b. Correlation
   c. Median
   d. Time series analysis

12. In statistics, _____ refers to techniques for the modeling and analysis of numerical data consisting of values of a dependent variable and of one or more independent variables The dependent variable in the regression equation is modeled as a function of the independent variables, corresponding parameters, and an error term. The error term is treated as a random variable and represents unexplained variation in the dependent variable.
   a. Regression analysis
   b. Trend analysis
   c. Stepwise regression
   d. Least squares

13. In statistics, the _____, R^2 is used in the context of statistical models whose main purpose is the prediction of future outcomes on the basis of other related information. It is the proportion of variability in a data set that is accounted for by the statistical model. It provides a measure of how well future outcomes are likely to be predicted by the model.
   a. Regression analysis
   b. Coefficient of determination
   c. Trend analysis
   d. Stepwise regression

14. The terms '_____' and 'independent variable' are used in similar but subtly different ways in mathematics and statistics as part of the standard terminology in those subjects. They are used to distinguish between two types of quantities being considered, separating them into those available at the start of a process and those being created by it, where the latter (_____s) are dependent on the former (independent variables.)

The independent variable is typically the variable being manipulated or changed and the _____ is the observed result of the independent variable being manipulated.

a. Dependent variable
b. 1990 Clean Air Act
c. 28-hour day
d. Taguchi methods

15. In statistics, _____ or explained randomness measures the proportion to which a mathematical model accounts for the variation (= apparent randomness) of a given data set. Often, variation is quantified as variance; then, the more specific term explained variance can be used.

The complementary part of the total variation/randomness/variance is called unexplained or residual.

a. A4e
b. A Stake in the Outcome
c. AAAI
d. Explained variation

16. In mathematics, the _____ of a real-valued function f, defined on an interval [a, b] $\subset$ R is a measure of the one-dimensional arclength of the curve with parametric equation x → f(x), for x ∈ [a,b]. The _____ of a continuously differentiable function can be given as the integral

$$V_b^a(f) = \int_a^b |f'(x)|\,dx.$$

The _____ of an arbitrary real valued function f defined on [a,b] is given by the more general formula

$$V_b^a(f) = \sup_P \sum_{i=0}^{n_p-1} |f(x_{i+1}) - f(x_i)|,$$

where the supremum runs over the set of all partitions P of the given interval.

The _____ of a real-valued integrable function f defined on a bounded domain $\Omega \subset \mathbb{R}^n$,

$$V(f, \Omega) := \sup\left\{\int_\Omega f \operatorname{div}\varphi : \varphi \in C_c^1(\Omega, \mathbb{R}^n),\ \|\varphi\|_{L^\infty(\Omega)} \leq 1\right\},$$

where $C_c^1(\Omega,\mathbb{R}^n)$ is the set of continuously differentiable vector functions of compact support contained in Ω (in particular Φ |$_{\delta\Omega}$ = 0), and $\|\cdot\|_{L^\infty(\Omega)}$ is the essential supremum norm.

a. 33 Strategies of War
b. 1990 Clean Air Act
c. 28-hour day
d. Total variation

17. In economics, _____s are key economic variables that economists used to predict a new phase of the business cycle. A _____ is one that changes before the economy does; a lagging indicator is one that changes after the economy has changed. Examples of _____s include stock prices, which often improve or worsen before a similar change in the economy.
   a. Perfect competition
   b. Leading indicator
   c. Deflation
   d. Human capital

18. In statistics, _____ includes regression models in which the choice of predictive variables is carried out by an automatic procedure. Usually, this takes the form of a sequence of F-tests, but other techniques are possible, such as t-tests, adjusted R-square, Akaike information criterion, Bayesian information criterion, Mallows' Cp, or false discovery rate. In this example from engineering, necessity and sufficiency are usually determined by F-tests.
   a. Stepwise regression
   b. Regression analysis
   c. Trend analysis
   d. Least squares

19. In probability theory and statistics, _____ is a measure of the variability or dispersion of a population, a data set, or a probability distribution. A low _____ indicates that the data points tend to be very close to the same value (the mean), while high _____ indicates that the data are 'spread out' over a large range of values.

For example, the average height for adult men in the United States is about 70 inches (178 cm), with a _____ of around 3 in (8 cm.)

   a. Normal distribution
   b. Failure rate
   c. Frequency distribution
   d. Standard deviation

20 *Chapter 3. Demand Forecasting*

20. In statistics, _____ is:

    - the arithmetic _____
    - the expected value of a random variable, which is also called the population _____.

It is sometimes stated that the '_____' _____s average. This is incorrect if '_____' is taken in the specific sense of 'arithmetic _____' as there are different types of averages: the _____, median, and mode. Other simple statistical analyses use measures of spread, such as range, interquartile range, or standard deviation. For a real-valued random variable X, the _____ is the expectation of X. Note that not every probability distribution has a defined _____; see the Cauchy distribution for an example.

   a. Mean
   b. Control chart
   c. Correlation
   d. Statistical inference

21. The _____ or simply average deviation of a data set is the average of the absolute deviations and is a summary statistic of statistical dispersion or variability. It is also called the mean absolute deviation, but this is easily confused with the median absolute deviation.

The average absolute deviation of a set $\{x_1, x_2, ..., x_n\}$ is

The choice of measure of central tendency, m(X), has a marked effect on the value of the average deviation.

   a. Average absolute deviation,
   b. A4e
   c. A Stake in the Outcome
   d. AAAI

22. In statistics, the _____ of an estimator is one of many ways to quantify the amount by which an estimator differs from the true value of the quantity being estimated. As a loss function, _____ is called squared error loss. _____ measures the average of the square of the 'error.' The error is the amount by which the estimator differs from the quantity to be estimated.

Chapter 3. Demand Forecasting 21

a. 1990 Clean Air Act
b. 28-hour day
c. 33 Strategies of War
d. Mean squared error

23. In statistics, a _____ rolling mean or running average, is a type of finite impulse response filter used to analyze a set of data points by creating a series of averages of different subsets of the full data set. A _____ is not a single number, but it is a set of numbers, each of which is the average of the corresponding subset of a larger set of data points. A _____ may also use unequal weights for each data value in the subset to emphasize particular values in the subset.
   a. Homoscedastic
   b. Moving average
   c. Standard deviation
   d. Time series analysis

24. In economics, _____ is the desire to own something and the ability to pay for it. The term _____ signifies the ability or the willingness to buy a particular commodity at a given point of time.
   a. Demand
   b. 33 Strategies of War
   c. 1990 Clean Air Act
   d. 28-hour day

25. In statistics, _____ is a technique that can be applied to time series data, either to produce smoothed data for presentation, or to make forecasts. The time series data themselves are a sequence of observations. The observed phenomenon may be an essentially random process, or it may be an orderly, but noisy, process.
   a. AAAI
   b. Exponential smoothing
   c. A Stake in the Outcome
   d. A4e

26. In statistics and image processing, to smooth a data set is to create an approximating function that attempts to capture important patterns in the data, while leaving out noise or other fine-scale structures/rapid phenomena. Many different algorithms are used in _____. One of the most common algorithms is the 'moving average', often used to try to capture important trends in repeated statistical surveys.

a. 1990 Clean Air Act
b. 28-hour day
c. 33 Strategies of War
d. Smoothing

27. An _____, sometimes also called an exponentially weighted moving average, applies weighting factors which decrease exponentially. The weighting for each older data point decreases exponentially, giving much more importance to recent observations while still not discarding older observations entirely. The graph at right shows an example of the weight decrease.
   a. A Stake in the Outcome
   b. Exponential moving average
   c. AAAI
   d. A4e

28. In economics, business, retail, and accounting, a _____ is the value of money that has been used up to produce something, and hence is not available for use anymore. In economics, a _____ is an alternative that is given up as a result of a decision. In business, the _____ may be one of acquisition, in which case the amount of money expended to acquire it is counted as _____.
   a. Fixed costs
   b. Cost overrun
   c. Cost allocation
   d. Cost

29. _____ is an advertisement in which a particular product specifically mentions a competitor by name for the express purpose of showing why the competitor is inferior to the product naming it.

This should not be confused with parody advertisements, where a fictional product is being advertised for the purpose of poking fun at the particular advertisement, nor should it be confused with the use of a coined brand name for the purpose of comparing the product without actually naming an actual competitor. ('Wikipedia tastes better and is less filling than the Encyclopedia Galactica.')

In the 1980s, during what has been referred to as the cola wars, soft-drink manufacturer Pepsi ran a series of advertisements where people, caught on hidden camera, in a blind taste test, chose Pepsi over rival Coca-Cola.

   a. 28-hour day
   b. Comparative advertising
   c. 33 Strategies of War
   d. 1990 Clean Air Act

30. An _____ is software that attempts to reproduce the performance of one or more human experts, most commonly in a specific problem domain, and is a traditional application and/or subfield of artificial intelligence. A wide variety of methods can be used to simulate the performance of the expert however common to most or all are 1) the creation of a so-called 'knowledgebase' which uses some knowledge representation formalism to capture the Subject Matter Experts (SME) knowledge and 2) a process of gathering that knowledge from the SME and codifying it according to the formalism, which is called knowledge engineering. _____s may or may not have learning components but a third common element is that once the system is developed it is proven by being placed in the same real world problem solving situation as the human SME, typically as an aid to human workers or a supplement to some information system.
   a. A Stake in the Outcome
   b. A4e
   c. Expert system
   d. AAAI

31. _____ is one of the managerial functions like planning, organizing, staffing and directing. It is an important function because it helps to check the errors and to take the corrective action so that deviation from standards are minimized and stated goals of the organization are achieved in desired manner. According to modern concepts, _____ is a foreseeing action whereas earlier concept of _____ was used only when errors were detected. _____ in management means setting standards, measuring actual performance and taking corrective action.
   a. Turnover
   b. Decision tree pruning
   c. Schedule of reinforcement
   d. Control

32. A _____ is a business that is privately owned and operated, with a small number of employees and relatively low volume of sales. The legal definition of 'small' often varies by country and industry, but is generally under 100 employees in the United States and under 50 employees in the European Union. In comparison, the definition of mid-sized business by the number of employees is generally under 500 in the U.S. and 250 for the European Union.
   a. Critical Success Factor
   b. Pre-determined overhead rate
   c. Golden Boot Compensation
   d. Small business

33. An _____ is a person who has possession of an enterprise and assumes significant accountability for the inherent risks and the outcome. It is an ambitious leader who combines land, labor, and capital to create and market new goods or services. The term is a loanword from French and was first defined by the Irish economist Richard Cantillon.

a. A4e
b. AAAI
c. A Stake in the Outcome
d. Entrepreneur

34. The _____ is the Cabinet department of the United States government concerned with promoting economic growth. It was originally created as the _____ and Labor on February 14, 1903. It was subsequently renamed to the Department of Commerce on March 4, 1913, and its bureaus and agencies specializing in labor were transferred to the new Department of Labor.

a. United States Department of Commerce
b. AAAI
c. A4e
d. A Stake in the Outcome

35. The _____ is a Cabinet department of the United States government responsible for occupational safety, wage and hour standards, unemployment insurance benefits, re-employment services, and some economic statistics. Many U.S. states also have such departments. The department is headed by the United States Secretary of Labor.

a. A4e
b. United States Department of Labor
c. A Stake in the Outcome
d. AAAI

Chapter 4. Product, Process, and Service Design

1. _____ is an advertisement in which a particular product specifically mentions a competitor by name for the express purpose of showing why the competitor is inferior to the product naming it.

This should not be confused with parody advertisements, where a fictional product is being advertised for the purpose of poking fun at the particular advertisement, nor should it be confused with the use of a coined brand name for the purpose of comparing the product without actually naming an actual competitor. ('Wikipedia tastes better and is less filling than the Encyclopedia Galactica.')

In the 1980s, during what has been referred to as the cola wars, soft-drink manufacturer Pepsi ran a series of advertisements where people, caught on hidden camera, in a blind taste test, chose Pepsi over rival Coca-Cola.

   a. 33 Strategies of War
   b. 1990 Clean Air Act
   c. Comparative advertising
   d. 28-hour day

2. The process of _____ involves the introduction of a good or service that is new or substantially improved. This includes, but is not limited to, improvements in functional characteristics, technical abilities, or ease of use.
   a. Job enlargement
   b. Service-profit chain
   c. Letter of resignation
   d. Product innovation

3. _____ is a term used in the movie and television industries to refer to the person responsible for the overall look of a filmed event such as films, TV programs, music videos or adverts. _____s have one of the key creative roles in the creation of motion pictures and television. Working directly with the director and producer, they must select the settings and style to visually tell the story.
   a. 28-hour day
   b. 1990 Clean Air Act
   c. 33 Strategies of War
   d. Production designer

4. _____ is a work methodology based on the parallelization of tasks (ie. concurrently.) It refers to an approach used in product development in which functions of design engineering, manufacturing engineering and other functions are integrated to reduce the elapsed time required to bring a new product to the market.
   a. Work package
   b. Critical Chain Project Management
   c. Project management
   d. Concurrent engineering

Chapter 4. Product, Process, and Service Design

5. A _____ is a type of business entity in which partners (owners) share with each other the profits or losses of the business. _____s are often favored over corporations for taxation purposes, as the _____ structure does not generally incur a tax on profits before it is distributed to the partners (i.e. there is no dividend tax levied.) However, depending on the _____ structure and the jurisdiction in which it operates, owners of a _____ may be exposed to greater personal liability than they would as shareholders of a corporation.
   a. Due process
   b. Mediation
   c. Partnership
   d. Federal Employers Liability Act

6. _____ can be defined as the idea generation, concept development, testing and manufacturing or implementation of a physical object or service. _____ers conceptualize and evaluate ideas, making them tangible through products in a more systematic approach. The role of a _____er encompasses many characteristics of the marketing manager, product manager, industrial designer and design engineer.
   a. Abraham Harold Maslow
   b. Affiliation
   c. Product design
   d. Adam Smith

7. In economics, _____ is the desire to own something and the ability to pay for it. The term _____ signifies the ability or the willingness to buy a particular commodity at a given point of time.
   a. 1990 Clean Air Act
   b. 28-hour day
   c. 33 Strategies of War
   d. Demand

8. _____ are parts that are for practical purposes identical. They are made to specifications that ensure that they are so nearly identical that they will fit into any device of the same type. One such part can freely replace another, without any custom fitting (such as filing.)
   a. A Stake in the Outcome
   b. A4e
   c. AAAI
   d. Interchangeable parts

9. In mathematical logic, _____ is a valid argument and rule of inference which makes the inference that, if the conjunction A and B is true, then A is true, and B is true.

In formal language:

$$A \wedge B \vdash A$$

or

$$A \wedge B \vdash B$$

The argument has one premise, namely a conjunction, and one often uses _____ in longer arguments to derive one of the conjuncts.

An example in English:

It's raining and it's pouring.

a. Validity
b. 1990 Clean Air Act
c. Fuzzy logic
d. Simplification

10. Engineering _____ is the permissible limit of variation in

1. a physical dimension,
2. a measured value or physical property of a material, manufactured object, system, or service,
3. other measured values (such as temperature, humidity, etc.)
4. in engineering and safety, a physical distance or space (_____), as in a truck (lorry), train or boat under a bridge as well as a train in a tunnel

Dimensions, properties, or conditions may vary within certain practical limits without significantly affecting functioning of equipment or a process. _____s are specified to allow reasonable leeway for imperfections and inherent variability without compromising performance.

The _____ may be specified as a factor or percentage of the nominal value, a maximum deviation from a nominal value, an explicit range of allowed values, be specified by a note or published standard with this information, or be implied by the numeric accuracy of the nominal value. _____ can be symmetrical, as in 40±0.1, or asymmetrical, such as 40+0.2/−0.1.

a. Quality assurance
b. Root cause analysis
c. Zero defects
d. Tolerance

11.

_____ is a systematic method to improve the 'value' of goods or products and services by using an examination of function. Value, as defined, is the ratio of function to cost. Value can therefore be increased by either improving the function or reducing the cost.

a. Capacity planning
b. Cellular manufacturing
c. Value engineering
d. Master production schedule

12. A _____ is a list of the general tasks and responsibilities of a position. Typically, it also includes to whom the position reports, specifications such as the qualifications needed by the person in the job, salary range for the position, etc. A _____ is usually developed by conducting a job analysis, which includes examining the tasks and sequences of tasks necessary to perform the job.

a. Recruitment
b. Job description
c. Recruitment advertising
d. Recruitment Process Insourcing

13. _____ is used for the design, development, analysis, and optimization of technical processes and is mainly applied to chemical plants and chemical processes, but also to power stations, and similar technical facilities. Process flow diagram of a typical amine treating process used in industrial plants

_____ is a model-based representation of chemical, physical, biological, and other technical processes and unit operations in software. Basic prerequisites are a thorough knowledge of chemical and physical properties of pure components and mixtures, of reactions, and of mathematical models which, in combination, allow the calculation of a process in computers.

a. 1990 Clean Air Act
b. Process simulation
c. 33 Strategies of War
d. 28-hour day

14. In microeconomics and management, the term _____ describes a style of management control. Vertically integrated companies are united through a hierarchy with a common owner. Usually each member of the hierarchy produces a different product or (market-specific) service, and the products combine to satisfy a common need.
   a. 28-hour day
   b. 33 Strategies of War
   c. 1990 Clean Air Act
   d. Vertical integration

15. _____ consists of the mental process of thinking involved with the process of judging the merits of multiple options and selecting one of them for action. Some simple examples include deciding whether to get up in the morning or go back to sleep, or selecting a given route for a journey. More complex examples (often decisions that affect what a person thinks or their core beliefs) include choosing a lifestyle, religious affiliation, or political position.
   a. Groups decision making
   b. Trade study
   c. Championship mobilization
   d. Choice

16. _____ is subcontracting a process, such as product design or manufacturing, to a third-party company. The decision to outsource is often made in the interest of lowering cost or making better use of time and energy costs, redirecting or conserving energy directed at the competencies of a particular business, or to make more efficient use of land, labor, capital, (information) technology and resources. _____ became part of the business lexicon during the 1980s.
   a. Outsourcing
   b. Opinion leadership
   c. Unemployment insurance
   d. Operant conditioning

17. _____ is the use of control systems (such as numerical control, programmable logic control, and other industrial control systems), in concert with other applications of information technology (such as computer-aided technologies [CAD, CAM, CAx]), to control industrial machinery and processes, reducing the need for human intervention. In the scope of industrialization, _____ is a step beyond mechanization. Whereas mechanization provided human operators with machinery to assist them with the physical requirements of work, _____ greatly reduces the need for human sensory and mental requirements as well.

a. A Stake in the Outcome
b. Automation
c. AAAI
d. A4e

18. Capital intensity is the term in economics for the amount of fixed or real capital present in relation to other factors of production, especially labor. At the level of either a production process or the aggregate economy, it may be estimated by the capital/labor ratio, such as from the points along a capital/labor isoquant.

Since the use of tools and machinery makes labor more effective, rising capital intensity (or 'capital deepening') pushes up the productivity of labor, so a society that is more _____ tends to have a higher standard of living over the long run than one with low capital intensity.

a. Cost of capital
b. 1990 Clean Air Act
c. Weighted average cost of capital
d. Capital intensive

19. An _____ is a manufacturing process in which parts (usually interchangeable parts) are added to a product in a sequential manner using optimally planned logistics to create a finished product much faster than with handcrafting-type methods. The _____ developed by Ford Motor Company between 1908 and 1915 made _____ s famous in the following decade through the social ramifications of mass production, such as the affordability of the Ford Model T and the introduction of high wages for Ford workers. However, the various preconditions for the development at Ford stretched far back into the 19th century, from the gradual realization of the dream of interchangeability, to the concept of reinventing workflow and job descriptions using analytical methods.

a. AAAI
b. A4e
c. A Stake in the Outcome
d. Assembly line

20. In probability theory, a probability distribution is called _____ if its cumulative distribution function is _____. This is equivalent to saying that for random variables X with the distribution in question, Pr[X = a] = 0 for all real numbers a, i.e.: the probability that X attains the value a is zero, for any number a. If the distribution of X is _____ then X is called a _____ random variable.

a. Pay Band
b. Continuous
c. Connectionist expert systems
d. Decision tree pruning

Chapter 4. Product, Process, and Service Design

21. A _____ is a set of sequential operations established in a factory whereby materials are put through a refining process to produce an end-product that is suitable for onward consumption; or components are assembled to make a finished article.

Typically, raw materials such as metal ores or agricultural products such as foodstuffs or textile source plants (cotton, flax) require a sequence of treatments to render them useful. For metal, the processes include crushing, smelting and further refining.

 a. Six Sigma
 b. Theory of constraints
 c. Takt time
 d. Production line

22. _____ are typically small manufacturing operations that handle specialized manufacturing processes such as small customer orders or small batch jobs. _____ typically move on to different jobs (possibly with different customers) when each job is completed. By nature of this type of manufacturing operation, _____ are usually specialized in skill and processes.
 a. 1990 Clean Air Act
 b. 28-hour day
 c. 33 Strategies of War
 d. Job shops

23. _____ is a model for workplace design, and is an integral part of lean manufacturing systems. The goal of lean manufacturing is the aggressive minimisation of waste, called muda, to achieve maximum efficiency of resources. _____, sometimes called cellular or cell production, arranges factory floor labor into semi-autonomous and multi-skilled teams, or work cells, who manufacture complete products or complex components.
 a. Remanufacturing
 b. Cellular manufacturing
 c. Scientific management
 d. Productivity

24. A _____ is typically described as a deliberate plan of action to guide decisions and achieve rational outcome(s.) However, the term may also be used to denote what is actually done, even though it is unplanned.

The term may apply to government, private sector organizations and groups, and individuals.

a. 28-hour day
b. 33 Strategies of War
c. 1990 Clean Air Act
d. Policy

25. In economics, business, retail, and accounting, a _____ is the value of money that has been used up to produce something, and hence is not available for use anymore. In economics, a _____ is an alternative that is given up as a result of a decision. In business, the _____ may be one of acquisition, in which case the amount of money expended to acquire it is counted as _____.
   a. Fixed costs
   b. Cost overrun
   c. Cost allocation
   d. Cost

26. _____ Management is the succession of strategies used by management as a product goes through its _____. The conditions in which a product is sold changes over time and must be managed as it moves through its succession of stages.

The _____ goes through many phases, involves many professional disciplines, and requires many skills, tools and processes.

   a. Golden handshake
   b. Job hunting
   c. Strategic Alliance
   d. Product life cycle

27. The 'business case for _____', theorizes that in a global marketplace, a company that employs a diverse workforce (both men and women, people of many generations, people from ethnically and racially diverse backgrounds etc.) is better able to understand the demographics of the marketplace it serves and is thus better equipped to thrive in that marketplace than a company that has a more limited range of employee demographics.

An additional corollary suggests that a company that supports the _____ of its workforce can also improve employee satisfaction, productivity and retention.

   a. Diversity
   b. Virtual team
   c. Trademark
   d. Kanban

Chapter 4. Product, Process, and Service Design

28. The _____ is a bank regulation, which sets a framework on how banks and depository institutions must handle their capital. The categorization of assets and capital is highly standardized so that it can be risk weighted. Internationally, the Basel Committee on Banking Supervision housed at the Bank for International Settlements influence each country's banking _____s.
   a. Lock box
   b. Reserve requirement
   c. Capital requirement
   d. 1990 Clean Air Act

29. In the fields of science, engineering, industry and statistics, _____ is the degree of closeness of a measured or calculated quantity to its actual (true) value. _____ is closely related to precision, also called reproducibility or repeatability, the degree to which further measurements or calculations show the same or similar results. _____ indicates proximity to the true value, precision to the repeatability or reproducibility of the measurement

The results of calculations or a measurement can be accurate but not precise, precise but not accurate, neither, or both.

   a. A Stake in the Outcome
   b. AAAI
   c. A4e
   d. Accuracy

30. _____ refers to an assessment of the viability, stability and profitability of a business, sub-business or project.

It is performed by professionals who prepare reports using ratios that make use of information taken from financial statements and other reports. These reports are usually presented to top management as one of their bases in making business decisions.

   a. 1990 Clean Air Act
   b. Financial analysis
   c. 28-hour day
   d. 33 Strategies of War

31. _____ is one of the four elements of marketing mix. An organization or set of organizations (go-betweens) involved in the process of making a product or service available for use or consumption by a consumer or business user.

The other three parts of the marketing mix are product, pricing, and promotion.

a. Distribution
b. Job creation programs
c. Missing completely at random
d. Matching theory

32. A _____ for a set of products is a warehouse or other specialized building, often with refrigeration or air conditioning, which is stocked with products (goods) to be re-distributed to retailers, wholesalers or directly to consumers. A _____ is a principle part, the 'order processing' element, of the entire 'order fulfillment' process. _____s are usually thought of as being 'demand driven'.
   a. Third-party logistics
   b. 28-hour day
   c. Distribution Center
   d. 1990 Clean Air Act

Chapter 5. Facility Capacity, Location, and Layout

1. _____ is the process of determining the production capacity needed by an organization to meet changing demands for its products. In the context of _____, 'capacity' is the maximum amount of work that an organization is capable of completing in a given period of time.

A discrepancy between the capacity of an organization and the demands of its customers results in inefficiency, either in under-utilized resources or unfulfilled customers.

   a. Remanufacturing
   b. Productivity
   c. Scientific management
   d. Capacity planning

2. _____ is a concept in economics which refers to the extent to which an enterprise or a nation actually uses its installed productive capacity. Thus, it refers to the relationship between actual output that 'is' produced with the installed equipment and the potential output which 'could' be produced with it, if capacity was fully used.

If market demand grows, _____ will rise.

   a. Diseconomies of scale
   b. Multifactor productivity
   c. Factors of production
   d. Capacity utilization

3. _____ is the process of estimation in unknown situations. Prediction is a similar, but more general term. Both can refer to estimation of time series, cross-sectional or longitudinal data.
   a. 33 Strategies of War
   b. 28-hour day
   c. 1990 Clean Air Act
   d. Forecasting

4. In economics, _____ is the desire to own something and the ability to pay for it. The term _____ signifies the ability or the willingness to buy a particular commodity at a given point of time.
   a. 28-hour day
   b. 1990 Clean Air Act
   c. 33 Strategies of War
   d. Demand

Chapter 5. Facility Capacity, Location, and Layout

5. _____ is the activity of estimating the quantity of a product or service that consumers will purchase. _____ involves techniques including both informal methods, such as educated guesses, and quantitative methods, such as the use of historical sales data or current data from test markets. _____ may be used in making pricing decisions, in assessing future capacity requirements, or in making decisions on whether to enter a new market.
   a. Profitability index
   b. 28-hour day
   c. 1990 Clean Air Act
   d. Demand Forecasting

6. In queueing theory, _____ is the proportion of the system's resources which is used by the traffic which arrives at it. It should be strictly less than one for the system to function well. It is usually represented by the symbol ρ.
   a. A Stake in the Outcome
   b. AAAI
   c. A4e
   d. Utilization

7. _____ are the forces that cause larger firms to produce goods and services at increased per-unit costs. They are less well known than what economists have long understood as 'economies of scale', the forces which enable larger firms to produce goods and services at reduced per-unit costs.

Some of the forces which cause a diseconomy of scale are listed below:

Ideally, all employees of a firm would have one-on-one communication with each other so they know exactly what the other workers are doing.

   a. Factors of production
   b. Multifactor productivity
   c. Production function
   d. Diseconomies of scale

8. Network externalities resemble economies of scale, but they are not considered such because they are a function of the number of users of a good or service in an industry, not of the production efficiency within a business. _____ are only considered examples of network externalities if they are driven by demand side economies.

Chapter 5. Facility Capacity, Location, and Layout

Formally, a production function is defined to have:

- constant returns to scale if (for any constant a greater than or equal to 0)
- increasing returns to scale if (for any constant a greater than 1)
- decreasing returns to scale if (for any constant a greater than 1)

where K and L are factors of production, capital and labour, respectively.

As an example, the Cobb-Douglas functional form has constant returns to scale when the sum of the exponents adds up to one.

a. A4e
b. A Stake in the Outcome
c. Economies of scale external to the firm
d. AAAI

9. In mathematics, _____ is a technique for optimization of a linear objective function, subject to linear equality and linear inequality constraints. Informally, _____ determines the way to achieve the best outcome (such as maximum profit or lowest cost) in a given mathematical model and given some list of requirements represented as linear equations.

More formally, given a polytope (for example, a polygon or a polyhedron), and a real-valued affine function

$$f(x_1, x_2, \ldots, x_n) = c_1 x_1 + c_2 x_2 + \cdots + c_n x_n + d$$

defined on this polytope, a _____ method will find a point in the polytope where this function has the smallest (or largest) value.

a. 1990 Clean Air Act
b. Linear programming relaxation
c. Linear programming
d. Slack variable

10. _____ is subcontracting a process, such as product design or manufacturing, to a third-party company. The decision to outsource is often made in the interest of lowering cost or making better use of time and energy costs, redirecting or conserving energy directed at the competencies of a particular business, or to make more efficient use of land, labor, capital, (information) technology and resources. _____ became part of the business lexicon during the 1980s.

a. Unemployment insurance
b. Operant conditioning
c. Opinion leadership
d. Outsourcing

11. A _____ is a decision support tool that uses a tree-like graph or model of decisions and their possible consequences, including chance event outcomes, resource costs, and utility. _____s are commonly used in operations research, specifically in decision analysis, to help identify a strategy most likely to reach a goal. Another use of _____s is as a descriptive means for calculating conditional probabilities.

a. 28-hour day
b. 1990 Clean Air Act
c. 33 Strategies of War
d. Decision tree

12. In probability theory and statistics, the _____ of a random variable is the integral of the random variable with respect to its probability measure. For discrete random variables this is equivalent to the probability-weighted sum of the possible values, and for continuous random variables with a density function it is the probability density -weighted integral of the possible values.

a. Expected value
b. AAAI
c. A4e
d. A Stake in the Outcome

13. _____ is a branch of operations research concerning itself with mathematical modeling and solution of problems concerning the placement of facilities in order to minimize transportation costs, avoid placing hazardous materials near housing, outperform competitors' facilities, etc.

A simple _____ problem is the Fermat-Weber problem, in which a single facility is to be placed, with the only optimization criterion being the minimization of the sum of distances from a given set of point sites. More complex problems considered in this discipline include the placement of multiple facilities, constraints on the locations of facilities, and more complex optimization criteria.

a. 28-hour day
b. Multiscale decision making
c. 1990 Clean Air Act
d. Facility location

Chapter 5. Facility Capacity, Location, and Layout

14. Capital intensity is the term in economics for the amount of fixed or real capital present in relation to other factors of production, especially labor. At the level of either a production process or the aggregate economy, it may be estimated by the capital/labor ratio, such as from the points along a capital/labor isoquant.

Since the use of tools and machinery makes labor more effective, rising capital intensity (or 'capital deepening') pushes up the productivity of labor, so a society that is more _____ tends to have a higher standard of living over the long run than one with low capital intensity.

   a. 1990 Clean Air Act
   b. Capital intensive
   c. Weighted average cost of capital
   d. Cost of capital

15. In economics and sociology, an _____ is any factor (financial or non-financial) that enables or motivates a particular course of action, or counts as a reason for preferring one choice to the alternatives. It is an expectation that encourages people to behave in a certain way. Since human beings are purposeful creatures, the study of _____ structures is central to the study of all economic activity (both in terms of individual decision-making and in terms of co-operation and competition within a larger institutional structure.)
   a. Incentive
   b. AAAI
   c. A Stake in the Outcome
   d. A4e

16. _____ consists of the sale of goods or merchandise from a fixed location, such as a department store, boutique or kiosk in small or individual lots for direct consumption by the purchaser. _____ may include subordinated services, such as delivery. Purchasers may be individuals or businesses.
   a. Planogram
   b. Retailing
   c. 28-hour day
   d. 1990 Clean Air Act

17. _____ is an advertisement in which a particular product specifically mentions a competitor by name for the express purpose of showing why the competitor is inferior to the product naming it.

This should not be confused with parody advertisements, where a fictional product is being advertised for the purpose of poking fun at the particular advertisement, nor should it be confused with the use of a coined brand name for the purpose of comparing the product without actually naming an actual competitor. ('Wikipedia tastes better and is less filling than the Encyclopedia Galactica.')

Chapter 5. Facility Capacity, Location, and Layout

In the 1980s, during what has been referred to as the cola wars, soft-drink manufacturer Pepsi ran a series of advertisements where people, caught on hidden camera, in a blind taste test, chose Pepsi over rival Coca-Cola.

a. 1990 Clean Air Act
b. Comparative advertising
c. 33 Strategies of War
d. 28-hour day

18. In economics, business, retail, and accounting, a _____ is the value of money that has been used up to produce something, and hence is not available for use anymore. In economics, a _____ is an alternative that is given up as a result of a decision. In business, the _____ may be one of acquisition, in which case the amount of money expended to acquire it is counted as _____.
    a. Cost overrun
    b. Fixed costs
    c. Cost allocation
    d. Cost

19. In the fields of science, engineering, industry and statistics, _____ is the degree of closeness of a measured or calculated quantity to its actual (true) value. _____ is closely related to precision, also called reproducibility or repeatability, the degree to which further measurements or calculations show the same or similar results. _____ indicates proximity to the true value, precision to the repeatability or reproducibility of the measurement

The results of calculations or a measurement can be accurate but not precise, precise but not accurate, neither, or both.

    a. A Stake in the Outcome
    b. A4e
    c. AAAI
    d. Accuracy

20. An _____ is a manufacturing process in which parts (usually interchangeable parts) are added to a product in a sequential manner using optimally planned logistics to create a finished product much faster than with handcrafting-type methods. The _____ developed by Ford Motor Company between 1908 and 1915 made _____s famous in the following decade through the social ramifications of mass production, such as the affordability of the Ford Model T and the introduction of high wages for Ford workers. However, the various preconditions for the development at Ford stretched far back into the 19th century, from the gradual realization of the dream of interchangeability, to the concept of reinventing workflow and job descriptions using analytical methods.

a. A4e
b. A Stake in the Outcome
c. AAAI
d. Assembly line

21. A _____ is a set of sequential operations established in a factory whereby materials are put through a refining process to produce an end-product that is suitable for onward consumption; or components are assembled to make a finished article.

Typically, raw materials such as metal ores or agricultural products such as foodstuffs or textile source plants (cotton, flax) require a sequence of treatments to render them useful. For metal, the processes include crushing, smelting and further refining.

a. Theory of constraints
b. Production line
c. Takt time
d. Six Sigma

22. _____ is a model for workplace design, and is an integral part of lean manufacturing systems. The goal of lean manufacturing is the aggressive minimisation of waste, called muda, to achieve maximum efficiency of resources. _____, sometimes called cellular or cell production, arranges factory floor labor into semi-autonomous and multi-skilled teams, or work cells, who manufacture complete products or complex components.

a. Remanufacturing
b. Scientific management
c. Cellular manufacturing
d. Productivity

23. The term '_____' refers to the concept of collecting information and attempting to spot a pattern in the information. In some fields of study, the term '_____' has more formally-defined meanings.

In project management _____ is a mathematical technique that uses historical results to predict future outcome.

a. Trend analysis
b. Least squares
c. Stepwise regression
d. Regression analysis

24. A _____ is a commercial building for storage of goods. _____s are used by manufacturers, importers, exporters, wholesalers, transport businesses, customs, etc. They are usually large plain buildings in industrial areas of cities and towns.
   a. 1990 Clean Air Act
   b. Warehouse
   c. 33 Strategies of War
   d. 28-hour day

25. _____ is an adjective for experience-based techniques that help in problem solving, learning and discovery. A _____ method is particularly used to rapidly come to a solution that is hoped to be close to the best possible answer, or 'optimal solution'. _____s are 'rules of thumb', educated guesses, intuitive judgments or simply common sense.
   a. 28-hour day
   b. 1990 Clean Air Act
   c. Representativeness
   d. Heuristic

Chapter 6. Operations Technologies

1. _____ is the use of control systems (such as numerical control, programmable logic control, and other industrial control systems), in concert with other applications of information technology (such as computer-aided technologies [CAD, CAM, CAx]), to control industrial machinery and processes, reducing the need for human intervention. In the scope of industrialization, _____ is a step beyond mechanization. Whereas mechanization provided human operators with machinery to assist them with the physical requirements of work, _____ greatly reduces the need for human sensory and mental requirements as well.
   a. AAAI
   b. Automation
   c. A Stake in the Outcome
   d. A4e

2. A _____ is a sensor able to detect the presence of nearby objects without any physical contact. A _____ often emits an electromagnetic or electrostatic field, or a beam of electromagnetic radiation (infrared, for instance), and looks for changes in the field or return signal. The object being sensed is often referred to as the _____'s target.
   a. 28-hour day
   b. Proximity sensor
   c. 1990 Clean Air Act
   d. 33 Strategies of War

3. _____ is one of the managerial functions like planning, organizing, staffing and directing. It is an important function because it helps to check the errors and to take the corrective action so that deviation from standards are minimized and stated goals of the organization are achieved in desired manner. According to modern concepts, _____ is a foreseeing action whereas earlier concept of _____ was used only when errors were detected. _____ in management means setting standards, measuring actual performance and taking corrective action.
   a. Turnover
   b. Decision tree pruning
   c. Control
   d. Schedule of reinforcement

4. In engineering and manufacturing, _____ and quality engineering are used in developing systems to ensure products or services are designed and produced to meet or exceed customer requirements. Refer to the definition by Merriam-Webster for further information . These systems are often developed in conjunction with other business and engineering disciplines using a cross-functional approach.
   a. Process capability
   b. Single Minute Exchange of Die
   c. Statistical process control
   d. Quality control

Chapter 6. Operations Technologies

5. A _____ is a computer program typically used to provide some form of artificial intelligence, which consists primarily of a set of rules about behavior. These rules, termed productions, are a basic representation found useful in AI planning, expert systems and action selection. A _____ provides the mechanism necessary to execute productions in order to achieve some goal for the system.

   a. 1990 Clean Air Act
   b. Production system
   c. 33 Strategies of War
   d. 28-hour day

6. A _____ system is a manufacturing system in which there is some amount of flexibility that allows the system to react in the case of changes, whether predicted or unpredicted. This flexibility is generally considered to fall into two categories, which both contain numerous subcategories.

The first category, machine flexibility, covers the system's ability to be changed to produce new product types, and ability to change the order of operations executed on a part. The second category is called routing flexibility, which consists of the ability to use multiple machines to perform the same operation on a part, as well as the system's ability to absorb large-scale changes, such as in volume, capacity, or capability.

   a. Manufacturing resource planning
   b. Flexible manufacturing
   c. Jidoka
   d. Homeworkers

7. _____ is a company-wide computer software system used to manage and coordinate all the resources, information, and functions of a business from shared data stores.

An _____ system has a service-oriented architecture with modular hardware and software units and 'services' that communicate on a local area network. The modular design allows a business to add or reconfigure modules (perhaps from different vendors) while preserving data integrity in one shared database that may be centralized or distributed.

   a. AAAI
   b. A4e
   c. A Stake in the Outcome
   d. Enterprise resource planning

Chapter 6. Operations Technologies

8. _____, commonly referred to as 'eBusiness' or 'e-Business', may be defined as the utilization of information and communication technologies (ICT) in support of all the activities of business. Commerce constitutes the exchange of products and services between businesses, groups and individuals and hence can be seen as one of the essential activities of any business. Hence, electronic commerce or eCommerce focuses on the use of ICT to enable the external activities and relationships of the business with individuals, groups and other businesses.

   a. AAAI
   b. A Stake in the Outcome
   c. Electronic business
   d. A4e

9. Manufacturing Resource Planning (_____) is defined by APICS as a method for the effective planning of all resources of a manufacturing company. Ideally, it addresses operational planning in units, financial planning in dollars, and has a simulation capability to answer 'what-if' questions and extension of closed-loop MRP. Manufacturing Resource Planning (or MRP2) - Around 1980, over-frequent changes in sales forecasts, entailing continual readjustments in production, as well as the unsuitability of the parameters fixed by the system, led MRP (Material Requirement Planning) to evolve into a new concept : Manufacturing Resource Planning (e.g. MRP 2)

This is not exclusively a software function, but a marriage of people skills, dedication to data base accuracy, and computer resources.

   a. Manufacturing resource planning
   b. Jidoka
   c. MRP II
   d. Homeworkers

10. _____ is an advertisement in which a particular product specifically mentions a competitor by name for the express purpose of showing why the competitor is inferior to the product naming it.

This should not be confused with parody advertisements, where a fictional product is being advertised for the purpose of poking fun at the particular advertisement, nor should it be confused with the use of a coined brand name for the purpose of comparing the product without actually naming an actual competitor. ('Wikipedia tastes better and is less filling than the Encyclopedia Galactica.')

In the 1980s, during what has been referred to as the cola wars, soft-drink manufacturer Pepsi ran a series of advertisements where people, caught on hidden camera, in a blind taste test, chose Pepsi over rival Coca-Cola.

   a. 33 Strategies of War
   b. 28-hour day
   c. 1990 Clean Air Act
   d. Comparative advertising

11. _____ is a concept in economics which refers to the extent to which an enterprise or a nation actually uses its installed productive capacity. Thus, it refers to the relationship between actual output that 'is' produced with the installed equipment and the potential output which 'could' be produced with it, if capacity was fully used.

If market demand grows, _____ will rise.

   a. Multifactor productivity
   b. Factors of production
   c. Diseconomies of scale
   d. Capacity utilization

12. In microeconomics, industrial organization is the field which describes the behavior of firms in the marketplace with regard to production, pricing, employment and other decisions. _____ in this field range from classical issues such as opportunity cost to neoclassical concepts such as factors of production.

- Production theory basics
    - production efficiency
    - factors of production
    - total, average, and marginal product curves
    - marginal productivity
    - isoquants ' isocosts
    - the marginal rate of technical substitution
- Economic rent
    - classical factor rents
    - Paretian factor rents
- Production possibility frontier
    - what products are possible given a set of resources
    - the trade-off between producing one product rather than another
    - the marginal rate of transformation
- Production function
    - inputs
    - diminishing returns to inputs
    - the stages of production
    - shifts in a production function
- Cost theory
    - the different types of costs
        - opportunity cost
        - accounting cost or historical costs
        - transaction cost
        - sunk cost
        - marginal cost
    - the isocost line
- Cost-of-production theory of value
- Long-run cost and production functions
    - long-run average cost
    - long-run production function and efficiency
    - returns to scale and isoclines
    - minimum efficient scale
    - plant capacity
- Economies of density
- Economies of scale
    - the efficiency consequences of increasing or decreasing the level of production
- Economies of scope
    - the efficiency consequences of increasing or decreasing the number of different types of products produced, promoted, and distributed
- Optimum factor allocation
    - output elasticity of factor costs
    - marginal revenue product
    - marginal resource cost
- Pricing
    - various aspects of the pricing decision
- Transfer pricing
    - selling within a multi-divisional company
- Joint product pricing
    - price setting when two products are linked
- Price discrimination

- - - different prices to different buyers
    - types of price discrimination
    - yield management
- Price skimming
  - price discrimination over time
- Two part tariffs
  - charging a price composed of two parts, usually an initial fee and an ongoing fee
- Price points
  - the effects of a non-linear demand curve on pricing
- Cost-plus pricing
  - a markup is applied to a cost term in order to calculate price
  - cost-plus pricing with elasticity considerations
  - cost plus pricing is often used along with break even analysis
- Rate of return pricing
  - calculate price based on the required rate of return on investment, or rate of return on sales
- Profit maximization
  - determining the optimum price and quantity
  - the totals approach
  - marginal approach of production

Chapter 6. Operations Technologies

a. Markup
b. Price floor
c. Pricing
d. Topics

13. _____ refers to the movement of cash into or out of a business or financial product. It is usually measured during a specified, finite period of time. Measurement of _____ can be used

- to determine a project's rate of return or value. The time of _____s into and out of projects are used as inputs in financial models such as internal rate of return, and net present value.
- to determine problems with a business's liquidity. Being profitable does not necessarily mean being liquid. A company can fail because of a shortage of cash, even while profitable.
- as an alternate measure of a business's profits when it is believed that accrual accounting concepts do not represent economic realities. For example, a company may be notionally profitable but generating little operational cash (as may be the case for a company that barters its products rather than selling for cash.) In such a case, the company may be deriving additional operating cash by issuing shares evaluating default risk, re-investment requirements, etc.

_____ is a generic term used differently depending on the context. It may be defined by users for their own purposes.

a. Gross profit
b. Gross profit margin
c. Sweat equity
d. Cash flow

14. _____ is the process of learning a new skill or trade, often in response to a change in the economic environment. Generally it reflects changes in profession choice rather than an 'upward' movement in the same field.

There is some controversy surrounding the use of _____ to offset economic changes caused by free trade and automation.

a. Compliance Training
b. Retraining
c. Krauthammer
d. Suspension training

15. A _____ is a business that is privately owned and operated, with a small number of employees and relatively low volume of sales. The legal definition of 'small' often varies by country and industry, but is generally under 100 employees in the United States and under 50 employees in the European Union. In comparison, the definition of mid-sized business by the number of employees is generally under 500 in the U.S. and 250 for the European Union.

Chapter 6. Operations Technologies

a. Small Business
b. Golden Boot Compensation
c. Critical Success Factor
d. Pre-determined overhead rate

16. The _____ is a United States government agency that provides support to small businesses.

The mission of the _____ is 'to maintain and strengthen the nation's economy by enabling the establishment and viability of small businesses and by assisting in the economic recovery of communities after disasters.'

The _____ makes loans directly to businesses and acts as a guarantor on bank loans. In some circumstances it also makes loans to victims of natural disasters, works to get government procurement contracts for small businesses, and assists businesses with management, technical and training issues.

a. 28-hour day
b. 33 Strategies of War
c. 1990 Clean Air Act
d. Small Business Administration

17. The _____ is the Cabinet department of the United States government concerned with promoting economic growth. It was originally created as the _____ and Labor on February 14, 1903. It was subsequently renamed to the Department of Commerce on March 4, 1913, and its bureaus and agencies specializing in labor were transferred to the new Department of Labor.
a. A4e
b. United States Department of Commerce
c. A Stake in the Outcome
d. AAAI

18. The _____ is a Cabinet department of the United States government responsible for occupational safety, wage and hour standards, unemployment insurance benefits, re-employment services, and some economic statistics. Many U.S. states also have such departments. The department is headed by the United States Secretary of Labor.
a. A Stake in the Outcome
b. United States Department of Labor
c. AAAI
d. A4e

19. A _____ is a set of categories designed to elicit information about a quantitative or a qualitative attribute. In the social sciences, common examples are the Likert scale and 1-10 _____s in which a person selects the number which is considered to reflect the perceived quality of a product.

A _____ is an instrument that requires the rater to assign the rated object that have numerals assigned to them.

   a. Thurstone scale
   b. Spearman-Brown prediction formula
   c. Polytomous Rasch model
   d. Rating scale

Chapter 7. Operations Quality Management

1. _____ can be considered to have three main components: quality control, quality assurance and quality improvement. _____ is focused not only on product quality, but also the means to achieve it. _____ therefore uses quality assurance and control of processes as well as products to achieve more consistent quality.
   a. 28-hour day
   b. Total quality management
   c. 1990 Clean Air Act
   d. Quality management

2. In economics, business, retail, and accounting, a _____ is the value of money that has been used up to produce something, and hence is not available for use anymore. In economics, a _____ is an alternative that is given up as a result of a decision. In business, the _____ may be one of acquisition, in which case the amount of money expended to acquire it is counted as _____.
   a. Cost allocation
   b. Cost overrun
   c. Fixed costs
   d. Cost

3. The concept of quality costs is a means to quantify the total _____-related efforts and deficiencies. It was first described by Armand V. Feigenbaum in a 1956 Harvard Business Review article.

   Prior to its introduction, the general perception was that higher quality requires higher costs, either by buying better materials or machines or by hiring more labor.

   a. Cost accounting
   b. Quality costs
   c. Fixed costs
   d. Cost of quality

4. _____ ('Plan-Do-Check-Act') is an iterative four-step problem-solving process typically used in business process improvement. It is also known as the Deming Cycle, Shewhart cycle, Deming Wheel, or Plan-Do-Study-Act.

   _____ was made popular by Dr. W. Edwards Deming, who is considered by many to be the father of modern quality control; however it was always referred to by him as the Shewhart cycle. Later in Deming's career, he modified _____ to Plan, Do, Study, Act (PDSA) so as to better describe his recommendations.

   a. PDCA
   b. Management by exception
   c. Management team
   d. Decentralization

Chapter 7. Operations Quality Management

5. _____ is one of the managerial functions like planning, organizing, staffing and directing. It is an important function because it helps to check the errors and to take the corrective action so that deviation from standards are minimized and stated goals of the organization are achieved in desired manner. According to modern concepts, _____ is a foreseeing action whereas earlier concept of _____ was used only when errors were detected. _____ in management means setting standards, measuring actual performance and taking corrective action.
   a. Schedule of reinforcement
   b. Control
   c. Turnover
   d. Decision tree pruning

6. In engineering and manufacturing, _____ and quality engineering are used in developing systems to ensure products or services are designed and produced to meet or exceed customer requirements. Refer to the definition by Merriam-Webster for further information . These systems are often developed in conjunction with other business and engineering disciplines using a cross-functional approach.
   a. Quality Control
   b. Statistical process control
   c. Process capability
   d. Single Minute Exchange of Die

7. A _____ is a volunteer group composed of workers (or even students), usually under the leadership of their supervisor (but they can elect a team leader), who are trained to identify, analyse and solve work-related problems and present their solutions to management in order to improve the performance of the organization, and motivate and enrich the work of employees. When matured, true _____s become self-managing, having gained the confidence of management. _____s are an alternative to the dehumanising concept of the Division of Labour, where workers or individuals are treated like robots.
   a. Competency-based job descriptions
   b. Connectionist expert systems
   c. Certified in Production and Inventory Management
   d. Quality circle

8. '_____' is Step 7 of 'Philip Crosby's 14 Step Quality Improvement Process' . Although applicable to any type of enterprise, it has been primarily adopted within industry supply chains wherever large volumes of components are being purchased (common items such as nuts and bolts are good examples.)

_____ was a quality control program originated by the Denver Division of the Martin Marietta Corporation (now Lockheed Martin) on the Titan Missile program, which carried the first astronauts into space in the late 1960s.

a. 28-hour day
b. 1990 Clean Air Act
c. Root cause analysis
d. Zero defects

9. _____ refers to metrics and measures of output from production processes, per unit of input. Labor _____, for example, is typically measured as a ratio of output per labor-hour, an input. _____ may be conceived of as a metrics of the technical or engineering efficiency of production.
   a. Productivity
   b. Value engineering
   c. Master production schedule
   d. Remanufacturing

10. _____ is an inventory strategy that strives to improve the return on investment of a business by reducing in-process inventory and its associated carrying costs. To meet _____ objectives, the process relies on signals between different points in the process. This means the process is often driven by a series of signals, or Kanban , which tell production when to make the next part. Kanban are usually 'tickets' but can be simple visual signals, such as the presence or absence of a part on a shelf. Implemented correctly, _____ can dramatically improve a manufacturing organization's return on investment, quality, and efficiency.
   a. 1990 Clean Air Act
   b. 28-hour day
   c. Just-in-time
   d. 33 Strategies of War

11. _____ or lean production, which is often known simply as 'Lean', is a production practice that considers the expenditure of resources for any goal other than the creation of value for the end customer to be wasteful, and thus a target for elimination. Working from the perspective of the customer who consumes a product or service, 'value' is defined as any action or process that a customer would be willing to pay for. Basically, lean is centered around creating more value with less work.
   a. Theory of constraints
   b. Six Sigma
   c. Production line
   d. Lean manufacturing

Chapter 7. Operations Quality Management

12. The _____ is given by the United States National Institute of Standards and Technology. Through the actions of the National Productivity Advisory Committee chaired by Jack Grayson, it was established by the Malcolm Baldrige National Quality Improvement Act of 1987 - Public Law 100-107 and named for Malcolm Baldrige, who served as United States Secretary of Commerce during the Reagan administration from 1981 until his 1987 death in a rodeo accident. APQC, , organized the first White House Conference on Productivity, spearheading the creation and design of the _____ in 1987, and jointly administering the award for its first three years.
    a. Scenario planning
    b. Time and attendance
    c. Malcolm Baldrige National Quality Award
    d. Business Network Transformation

13. _____ has the following meanings:

The care and servicing by personnel for the purpose of maintaining equipment and facilities in satisfactory operating condition by providing for systematic inspection, detection, and correction of incipient failures either before they occur or before they develop into major defects.

  1. Maintenance, including tests, measurements, adjustments, and parts replacement, performed specifically to prevent faults from occurring.

While _____ is generally considered to be worthwhile, there are risks such as equipment failure or human error involved when performing _____, just as in any maintenance operation. _____ as scheduled overhaul or scheduled replacement provides two of the three proactive failure management policies available to the maintenance engineer. Common methods of determining what _____ failure management policies should be applied are; OEM recommendations, requirements of codes and legislation within a jurisdiction, what an 'expert' thinks ought to be done, or the maintenance that's already done to similar equipment.

   a. 1990 Clean Air Act
   b. 33 Strategies of War
   c. Preventive maintenance
   d. 28-hour day

14. The _____, widely known as ISO , is an international-standard-setting body composed of representatives from various national standards organizations. Founded on 23 February 1947, the organization promulgates worldwide proprietary industrial and commercial standards. It is headquartered in Geneva, Switzerland.
    a. International Organization for Standardization
    b. A Stake in the Outcome
    c. AAAI
    d. A4e

Chapter 7. Operations Quality Management

15. _____ has been described as the 'process of social influence in which one person can enlist the aid and support of others in the accomplishment of a common task'. A definition more inclusive of followers comes from Alan Keith of Genentech who said '_____ is ultimately about creating a way for people to contribute to making something extraordinary happen.'

_____ is one of the most salient aspects of the organizational context. However, defining _____ has been challenging.

 a. Leadership
 b. Situational leadership
 c. 28-hour day
 d. 1990 Clean Air Act

16. _____ is a business management strategy, initially implemented by Motorola, that today enjoys widespread application in many sectors of industry.

_____ seeks to improve the quality of process outputs by identifying and removing the causes of defects (errors) and variation in manufacturing and business processes. It uses a set of quality management methods, including statistical methods, and creates a special infrastructure of people within the organization ('Black Belts' etc.)

 a. Production line
 b. Six Sigma
 c. Theory of constraints
 d. Takt time

17. A _____ is a form of qualitative research in which a group of people are asked about their attitude towards a product, service, concept, advertisement, idea, or packaging. Questions are asked in an interactive group setting where participants are free to talk with other group members.

The first _____s were created at the Bureau of Applied Social Research by associate director, sociologist Robert K. Merton.

 a. Marketing research
 b. Focus group
 c. Market analysis
 d. 1990 Clean Air Act

Chapter 7. Operations Quality Management

18. _____ is a 'method to transform user demands into design quality, to deploy the functions forming quality, and to deploy methods for achieving the design quality into subsystems and component parts, and ultimately to specific elements of the manufacturing process.' , as described by Dr. Yoji Akao, who originally developed _____ in Japan in 1966, when the author combined his work in quality assurance and quality control points with function deployment used in Value Engineering.

_____ is designed to help planners focus on characteristics of a new or existing product or service from the viewpoints of market segments, company, or technology-development needs. The technique yields graphs and matrices.

   a. 1990 Clean Air Act
   b. Hoshin Kanri
   c. Learning organization
   d. Quality function deployment

19. A _____ is a list of the general tasks and responsibilities of a position. Typically, it also includes to whom the position reports, specifications such as the qualifications needed by the person in the job, salary range for the position, etc. A _____ is usually developed by conducting a job analysis, which includes examining the tasks and sequences of tasks necessary to perform the job.
   a. Recruitment advertising
   b. Recruitment
   c. Recruitment Process Insourcing
   d. Job description

20. In mathematical logic, _____ is a valid argument and rule of inference which makes the inference that, if the conjunction A and B is true, then A is true, and B is true.

In formal language:

$$A \wedge B \vdash A$$

or

$$A \wedge B \vdash B$$

The argument has one premise, namely a conjunction, and one often uses _____ in longer arguments to derive one of the conjuncts.

An example in English:

   It's raining and it's pouring.

a. Validity
b. Simplification
c. Fuzzy logic
d. 1990 Clean Air Act

21. A _____ is a type of business entity in which partners (owners) share with each other the profits or losses of the business. _____s are often favored over corporations for taxation purposes, as the _____ structure does not generally incur a tax on profits before it is distributed to the partners (i.e. there is no dividend tax levied.) However, depending on the _____ structure and the jurisdiction in which it operates, owners of a _____ may be exposed to greater personal liability than they would as shareholders of a corporation.
   a. Mediation
   b. Federal Employers Liability Act
   c. Due process
   d. Partnership

22. The _____ is a measurable property of a process to the specification, expressed as a _____ index (e.g., C_{pk} or C_{pm}) or as a process performance index (e.g., P_{pk} or P_{pm}.) The output of this measurement is usually illustrated by a histogram and calculations that predict how many parts will be produced out of specification.

_____ is also defined as the capability of a process to meet its purpose as managed by an organization's management and process definition structures ISO 15504.

   a. Quality control
   b. Single Minute Exchange of Die
   c. Statistical process control
   d. Process capability

23. In process improvement efforts, the _____ or process capability ratio is a statistical measure of process capability: The ability of a process to produce output within engineering tolerances and specification limits. The concept of process capability only holds meaning for processes that are in a state of statistical control.

If the upper and lower specifications of the process are USL and LSL, the target process mean is T, the estimated mean of the process is $\hat{\mu}$ and the estimated variability of the process (expressed as a standard deviation) is $\hat{\sigma}$, then commonly-accepted process capability indices include:

$\hat{\sigma}$ is estimated using the sample standard deviation.

a. Process capability index
b. Process capability ratio
c. 1990 Clean Air Act
d. Constant dollars

24. _____ is the provision of service to customers before, during and after a purchase.

According to Turban et al. (2002), '_____ is a series of activities designed to enhance the level of customer satisfaction - that is, the feeling that a product or service has met the customer expectation.'

Its importance varies by product, industry and customer; defective or broken merchandise can be exchanged, often only with a receipt and within a specified time frame.

a. 1990 Clean Air Act
b. 28-hour day
c. Service rate
d. Customer service

25. _____ is one of the four elements of marketing mix. An organization or set of organizations (go-betweens) involved in the process of making a product or service available for use or consumption by a consumer or business user.

The other three parts of the marketing mix are product, pricing, and promotion.

a. Missing completely at random
b. Distribution
c. Job creation programs
d. Matching theory

26. _____ is an advertisement in which a particular product specifically mentions a competitor by name for the express purpose of showing why the competitor is inferior to the product naming it.

This should not be confused with parody advertisements, where a fictional product is being advertised for the purpose of poking fun at the particular advertisement, nor should it be confused with the use of a coined brand name for the purpose of comparing the product without actually naming an actual competitor. ('Wikipedia tastes better and is less filling than the Encyclopedia Galactica.')

In the 1980s, during what has been referred to as the cola wars, soft-drink manufacturer Pepsi ran a series of advertisements where people, caught on hidden camera, in a blind taste test, chose Pepsi over rival Coca-Cola.

a. 1990 Clean Air Act
b. 33 Strategies of War
c. 28-hour day
d. Comparative advertising

27. _____ refers to increasing the spiritual, political, social or economic strength of individuals and communities. It often involves the empowered developing confidence in their own capacities.

The term Human _____ covers a vast landscape of meanings, interpretations, definitions and disciplines ranging from psychology and philosophy to the highly commercialized Self-Help industry and Motivational sciences.

a. A4e
b. AAAI
c. A Stake in the Outcome
d. Empowerment

28. _____ is the process of comparing the cost, cycle time, productivity, or quality of a specific process or method to another that is widely considered to be an industry standard or best practice. Essentially, _____ provides a snapshot of the performance of your business and helps you understand where you are in relation to a particular standard. The result is often a business case for making changes in order to make improvements.
a. Complementors
b. Competitive heterogeneity
c. Cost leadership
d. Benchmarking

29. In probability theory, a probability distribution is called _____ if its cumulative distribution function is _____. This is equivalent to saying that for random variables X with the distribution in question, Pr[X = a] = 0 for all real numbers a, i.e.: the probability that X attains the value a is zero, for any number a. If the distribution of X is _____ then X is called a _____ random variable.
a. Connectionist expert systems
b. Pay Band
c. Decision tree pruning
d. Continuous

30. _____ is a management process whereby delivery (customer valued) processes are constantly evaluated and improved in the light of their efficiency, effectiveness and flexibility.

Some see it as a meta process for most management systems (Business Process Management, Quality Management, Project Management). Deming saw it as part of the 'system' whereby feedback from the process and customer were evaluated against organisational goals.

   a. Sole proprietorship
   b. Continuous Improvement Process
   c. Critical Success Factor
   d. First-mover advantage

31. _____ is a business management strategy aimed at embedding awareness of quality in all organizational processes. _____ has been widely used in manufacturing, education, hospitals, call centers, government, and service industries, as well as NASA space and science programs.

As defined by the International Organization for Standardization (ISO):

   '_____ is a management approach for an organization, centered on quality, based on the participation of all its members and aiming at long-term success through customer satisfaction, and benefits to all members of the organization and to society.' ISO 8402:1994

One major aim is to reduce variation from every process so that greater consistency of effort is obtained. (Royse, D., Thyer, B., Padgett D., ' Logan T., 2006)

   a. Total quality management
   b. 1990 Clean Air Act
   c. Quality management
   d. 28-hour day

Chapter 8. Strategic Allocation of Resources

1. _____ in the USA, Canada, South Africa and Australia, and operational research in Europe, is an interdisciplinary branch of applied mathematics and formal science that uses methods such as mathematical modeling, statistics, and algorithms to arrive at optimal or near optimal solutions to complex problems. It is typically concerned with optimizing the maxima (profit, assembly line performance, crop yield, bandwidth, etc) or minima (loss, risk, etc.) of some objective function.
   a. A4e
   b. A Stake in the Outcome
   c. AAAI
   d. Operations research

2. In mathematics, _____ is a technique for optimization of a linear objective function, subject to linear equality and linear inequality constraints. Informally, _____ determines the way to achieve the best outcome (such as maximum profit or lowest cost) in a given mathematical model and given some list of requirements represented as linear equations.

   More formally, given a polytope (for example, a polygon or a polyhedron), and a real-valued affine function

   $$f(x_1, x_2, \ldots, x_n) = c_1 x_1 + c_2 x_2 + \cdots + c_n x_n + d$$

   defined on this polytope, a _____ method will find a point in the polytope where this function has the smallest (or largest) value.

   a. Slack variable
   b. Linear programming
   c. 1990 Clean Air Act
   d. Linear programming relaxation

3. _____ is a Fortune 500, American multinational corporation headquartered in Cincinnati, Ohio, that manufactures a wide range of consumer goods. As of 2008, P'G is the 8th largest corporation in the world by market capitalization and 14th largest US company by profit.
   a. Maturity of Organizations and Business Excellence - The Four-Phase Model
   b. STAR
   c. Turnover
   d. Procter ' Gamble Co.

4. _____ is an area of business concerned with the production of goods and services, and involves the responsibility of ensuring that business operations are efficient in terms of using as little resource as needed, and effective in terms of meeting customer requirements. It is concerned with managing the process that converts inputs (in the forms of materials, labour and energy) into outputs (in the form of goods and services.)

Chapter 8. Strategic Allocation of Resources

Operations traditionally refers to the production of goods and services separately, although the distinction between these two main types of operations is increasingly difficult to make as manufacturers tend to merge product and service offerings.

　a. AAAI
　b. Operations management
　c. A Stake in the Outcome
　d. A4e

5. In economics, business, retail, and accounting, a _____ is the value of money that has been used up to produce something, and hence is not available for use anymore. In economics, a _____ is an alternative that is given up as a result of a decision. In business, the _____ may be one of acquisition, in which case the amount of money expended to acquire it is counted as _____.
　a. Cost allocation
　b. Fixed costs
　c. Cost
　d. Cost overrun

6. An unrelated, but similarly named method is the Nelder-Mead method or downhill _____ due to Nelder ' Mead (1965) and is a numerical method for optimizing many-dimensional unconstrained problems, belonging to the more general class of search algorithms.

In both cases, the method uses the concept of a simplex, which is a polytope of N + 1 vertices in N dimensions: a line segment in one dimension, a triangle in two dimensions, a tetrahedron in three-dimensional space and so forth.

A system of linear inequalities defines a polytope as a feasible region.
　a. 1990 Clean Air Act
　b. 28-hour day
　c. 33 Strategies of War
　d. Simplex method

7. The _____ is one of the fundamental combinatorial optimization problems in the branch of optimization or operations research in mathematics. It consists of finding a maximum weight matching in a weighted bipartite graph.

In its most general form, the problem is as follows:

　　There are a number of agents and a number of tasks.

a. AAAI
b. A4e
c. A Stake in the Outcome
d. Assignment problem

8. In Linear programming a _____ is a variable that is added to a constraint to turn the inequality into an equation. This is required to turn an inequality into an equality where a linear combination of variables is less than or equal to a given constant in the former. As with the other variables in the augmented constraints, the _____ cannot take on negative values, as the Simplex algorithm requires them to be positive or zero.
   a. Linear programming relaxation
   b. 1990 Clean Air Act
   c. Nonlinear programming
   d. Slack variable

Chapter 9. Service Operations Planning and Scheduling

1. _____ is an advertisement in which a particular product specifically mentions a competitor by name for the express purpose of showing why the competitor is inferior to the product naming it.

This should not be confused with parody advertisements, where a fictional product is being advertised for the purpose of poking fun at the particular advertisement, nor should it be confused with the use of a coined brand name for the purpose of comparing the product without actually naming an actual competitor. ('Wikipedia tastes better and is less filling than the Encyclopedia Galactica.')

In the 1980s, during what has been referred to as the cola wars, soft-drink manufacturer Pepsi ran a series of advertisements where people, caught on hidden camera, in a blind taste test, chose Pepsi over rival Coca-Cola.

   a. 1990 Clean Air Act
   b. 33 Strategies of War
   c. 28-hour day
   d. Comparative advertising

2. In economics, _____ is the desire to own something and the ability to pay for it. The term _____ signifies the ability or the willingness to buy a particular commodity at a given point of time.
   a. 1990 Clean Air Act
   b. 28-hour day
   c. Demand
   d. 33 Strategies of War

3. _____ is an adjective for experience-based techniques that help in problem solving, learning and discovery. A _____ method is particularly used to rapidly come to a solution that is hoped to be close to the best possible answer, or 'optimal solution'. _____s are 'rules of thumb', educated guesses, intuitive judgments or simply common sense.
   a. 28-hour day
   b. Representativeness
   c. 1990 Clean Air Act
   d. Heuristic

4. _____ of the learning curve effect and the closely related experience curve effect express the relationship between equations for experience and efficiency or between efficiency gains and investment in the effort. The experience of 'learning curves' was first observed by the 19th Century German psychologist Hermann Ebbinghaus according to the difficulty of memorizing varying numbers of verbal stimuli, and subsequent learning about the complex processes of learning are discussed in the

.

The rule used for representing the learning curve effect states that the more times a task has been performed, the less time will be required on each subsequent iteration.

Chapter 9. Service Operations Planning and Scheduling

a. Spatial Decision Support Systems
b. Distribution
c. Models
d. Point biserial correlation coefficient

5. _____ is an area of business concerned with the production of goods and services, and involves the responsibility of ensuring that business operations are efficient in terms of using as little resource as needed, and effective in terms of meeting customer requirements. It is concerned with managing the process that converts inputs (in the forms of materials, labour and energy) into outputs (in the form of goods and services.)

Operations traditionally refers to the production of goods and services separately, although the distinction between these two main types of operations is increasingly difficult to make as manufacturers tend to merge product and service offerings.

a. Operations management
b. A Stake in the Outcome
c. AAAI
d. A4e

6. _____-model (SCOR(r)) is a process reference model developed by the management consulting firm PRTM and AMR Research and endorsed by the Supply-Chain Council (SCC) as the cross-industry de facto standard diagnostic tool for supply chain management. SCOR enables users to address, improve, and communicate supply chain management practices within and between all interested parties in the Extended Enterprise.

SCOR(r) is a management tool, spanning from the supplier's supplier to the customer's customer. The model has been developed by the members of the Council on a volunteer basis to describe the business activities associated with all phases of satisfying a customer's demand.

a. Supply chain management software
b. Supply Chain Risk Management
c. Delayed differentiation
d. Supply-Chain Operations Reference

Chapter 10. Project Management

1. _____ refers to the movement of cash into or out of a business or financial product. It is usually measured during a specified, finite period of time. Measurement of _____ can be used

    - to determine a project's rate of return or value. The time of _____s into and out of projects are used as inputs in financial models such as internal rate of return, and net present value.
    - to determine problems with a business's liquidity. Being profitable does not necessarily mean being liquid. A company can fail because of a shortage of cash, even while profitable.
    - as an alternate measure of a business's profits when it is believed that accrual accounting concepts do not represent economic realities. For example, a company may be notionally profitable but generating little operational cash (as may be the case for a company that barters its products rather than selling for cash.) In such a case, the company may be deriving additional operating cash by issuing shares evaluating default risk, re-investment requirements, etc.

    _____ is a generic term used differently depending on the context. It may be defined by users for their own purposes.

    a. Cash flow
    b. Gross profit margin
    c. Gross profit
    d. Sweat equity

2. _____ is the discipline of planning, organizing and managing resources to bring about the successful completion of specific project goals and objectives. It is often closely related to and sometimes conflated with Program management.

    A project is a finite endeavor--having specific start and completion dates--undertaken to meet particular goals and objectives, usually to bring about beneficial change or added value.

    a. Work package
    b. Precedence diagram
    c. Project management
    d. Project engineer

3. _____ is one of the managerial functions like planning, organizing, staffing and directing. It is an important function because it helps to check the errors and to take the corrective action so that deviation from standards are minimized and stated goals of the organization are achieved in desired manner. According to modern concepts, _____ is a foreseeing action whereas earlier concept of _____ was used only when errors were detected. _____ in management means setting standards, measuring actual performance and taking corrective action.
    a. Turnover
    b. Schedule of reinforcement
    c. Control
    d. Decision tree pruning

Chapter 10. Project Management

4. The _____ in statistical process control is a tool used to determine whether a manufacturing or business process is in a state of statistical control or not.

If the chart indicates that the process is currently under control then it can be used with confidence to predict the future performance of the process. If the chart indicates that the process being monitored is not in control, the pattern it reveals can help determine the source of variation to be eliminated to bring the process back into control.

   a. Time series analysis
   b. Simple moving average
   c. Control chart
   d. Failure rate

5. The _____ is a non-profit professional organization with the purpose of advancing the state-of-the-art of project management. The company is a professional association for the project management profession.

The _____ Inc.

   a. 28-hour day
   b. 33 Strategies of War
   c. 1990 Clean Air Act
   d. Project Management Institute

6. _____ is a credential offered by the Project Management Institute (PMI.) The credential is obtained by documenting your work experience in project management, completing 35 hours of project management related training, and scoring at least 61% on a written, multiple choice examination. _____ exams administered on or before June 30, 2009 will be based on 'A Guide to the Project Management Body of Knowledge - or PMBOK,' the Third Edition.
   a. 1990 Clean Air Act
   b. Project Management Professional
   c. 33 Strategies of War
   d. 28-hour day

7. _____ are conventions, treaties and recommendations designed to eliminate unjust and inhumane labour practices. The primary inernational agency charged with developing such standards is the International Labour Organization (ILO.) Established in 1919, the ILO advocates international standards as essential for the eradication of labour conditions involving 'injustice, hardship and privation'.

Chapter 10. Project Management

a. Anaconda Copper
b. Airbus Industrie
c. International labour standards
d. Airbus SAS

8. The phrase mergers and _____s refers to the aspect of corporate strategy, corporate finance and management dealing with the buying, selling and combining of different companies that can aid, finance, or help a growing company in a given industry grow rapidly without having to create another business entity.

An _____, also known as a takeover or a buyout, is the buying of one company (the 'target') by another. An _____ may be friendly or hostile.

a. AAAI
b. Acquisition
c. A Stake in the Outcome
d. A4e

9. The _____, is a mathematically based algorithm for scheduling a set of project activities. It is an important tool for effective project management.

It was developed in the 1950s by the Dupont Corporation at about the same time that General Dynamics and the US Navy were developing the Program Evaluation and Review Technique (PERT) Today, it is commonly used with all forms of projects, including construction, software development, research projects, product development, engineering, and plant maintenance, among others.

a. 1990 Clean Air Act
b. 33 Strategies of War
c. Critical path method
d. 28-hour day

10. The Program (or Project) Evaluation and Review Technique, commonly abbreviated _____, is a model for project management designed to analyze and represent the tasks involved in completing a given project.

_____ is a method to analyze the involved tasks in completing a given project, specially the time needed to complete each task, and identifying the minimum time needed to complete the total project.

_____ was developed primarily to simplify the planning and scheduling of large and complex projects.

a. 28-hour day
b. 33 Strategies of War
c. 1990 Clean Air Act
d. PERT

11. A _____ is a subset of the overall internal controls of a business covering the application of people, documents, technologies, and procedures by management accountants to solving business problems such as costing a product, service or a business-wide strategy. _____s are distinct from regular information systems in that they are used to analyze other information systems applied in operational activities in the organization. Academically, the term is commonly used to refer to the group of information management methods tied to the automation or support of human decision making, e.g. Decision Support Systems, Expert systems, and Executive information systems.

a. 28-hour day
b. Strategic information system
c. 1990 Clean Air Act
d. Management information system

12. In physics, and more specifically kinematics, _____ is the change in velocity over time. Because velocity is a vector, it can change in two ways: a change in magnitude and/or a change in direction. In one dimension, _____ is the rate at which something speeds up or slows down.

a. AAAI
b. A Stake in the Outcome
c. A4e
d. Acceleration

13. _____ is a project management software program that is used for planning, tracking, and reporting project goals. The application enables users to organize tasks into project plans, assign resources to tasks, and view project details in Gantt charts, monthly calendars, and resource histograms.

_____'s capabilities are suited for project management beginners as well as experienced project managers working in small to mid-sized project teams.

a. 33 Strategies of War
b. 28-hour day
c. 1990 Clean Air Act
d. FastTrack Schedule

14. _____ is the process of estimation in unknown situations. Prediction is a similar, but more general term. Both can refer to estimation of time series, cross-sectional or longitudinal data.

a. 33 Strategies of War
b. Forecasting
c. 1990 Clean Air Act
d. 28-hour day

15. A _____ is a type of bar chart that illustrates a project schedule. _____s illustrate the start and finish dates of the terminal elements and summary elements of a project. Terminal elements and summary elements comprise the work breakdown structure of the project.

a. 28-hour day
b. 33 Strategies of War
c. Gantt chart
d. 1990 Clean Air Act

16. A _____ is a graph (flow chart) depicting the sequence in which a project's terminal elements are to be completed by showing terminal elements and their dependencies.

The work breakdown structure or the product breakdown structure show the 'part-whole' relations. In contrast, the _____ shows the 'before-after' relations.

a. 33 Strategies of War
b. 1990 Clean Air Act
c. 28-hour day
d. Project network

Chapter 11. Supply Chain Management and E-Business

1. A _____ is the system of organizations, people, technology, activities, information and resources involved in moving a product or service from supplier to customer. _____ activities transform natural resources, raw materials and components into a finished product that is delivered to the end customer. In sophisticated _____ systems, used products may re-enter the _____ at any point where residual value is recyclable.
   a. Wholesalers
   b. Drop shipping
   c. Supply chain
   d. Packaging

2. _____ is the management of a network of interconnected businesses involved in the ultimate provision of product and service packages required by end customers (Harland, 1996.) _____ spans all movement and storage of raw materials, work-in-process inventory, and finished goods from point of origin to point of consumption (supply chain.)

   The definition an American professional association put forward is that _____ encompasses the planning and management of all activities involved in sourcing, procurement, conversion, and logistics management activities.

   a. Packaging
   b. Drop shipping
   c. Freight forwarder
   d. Supply chain management

3. _____ is the management of the flow of goods, information and other resources, including energy and people, between the point of origin and the point of consumption in order to meet the requirements of consumers (frequently, and originally, military organizations.) _____ involves the integration of information, transportation, inventory, warehousing, material-handling, and packaging, and occasionally security. _____ is a channel of the supply chain which adds the value of time and place utility.
   a. 1990 Clean Air Act
   b. Third-party logistics
   c. 28-hour day
   d. Logistics

4. The term _____ is that part of Supply Chain Management that plans, implements, and controls the efficient, effective, forward, and reverse flow and storage of goods, services, and related information between the point of origin and the point of consumption in order to meet customers' requirements.

Software is used for logistics automation which helps the supply chain industry in automating the work flow as well as management of the system. There are very few generalized software available in the new market in the said topology.

a. Dynamic Enterprise Modeling
b. Micromanagement
c. Logistics management
d. Contingency theory

5. An _____, or organogram(me)) is a diagram that shows the structure of an organization and the relationships and relative ranks of its parts and positions/jobs. The term is also used for similar diagrams, for example ones showing the different elements of a field of knowledge or a group of languages. The French Encyclopédie had one of the first _____s of knowledge in general.
    a. Organizational chart
    b. AAAI
    c. A4e
    d. A Stake in the Outcome

6. _____ describes commerce transactions between businesses, such as between a manufacturer and a wholesaler, or between a wholesaler and a retailer. Contrasting terms are business-to-consumer (B2C) and business-to-government (B2G.)

The volume of B2B transactions is much higher than the volume of B2C transactions.

   a. Product bundling
   b. Category management
   c. Market environment
   d. Business-to-business

7. A _____ is an employee within a company, business or other organization who is responsible at some level for buying or approving the acquisition of goods and services needed by the company. The position responsibilities may be the same as that of a buyer or purchasing agent, or may include wider supervisory or managerial responsibilities. A _____ may oversee the acquisition of materials needed for production, general supplies for offices and facilities, equipment, or construction contracts.
    a. CEO
    b. Director of communications
    c. Financial analyst
    d. Purchasing manager

8. As part of an organization's internal financial controls, the accounting department may institute a _____ process to help manage requests for purchases. Requests for the creation of purchase of goods and services are documented and routed for approval within the organization and then delivered to the accounting group.

Chapter 11. Supply Chain Management and E-Business

Typically an accounting staff member is assigned responsibility for purchase order management, referred to commonly as the PO (purchase order) Coordinator.

a. Purchase requisition
b. Request for quotation
c. 1990 Clean Air Act
d. Purchasing process

9.

The _____ can vary from one organization to another but there are some key elements that are common throughout

The process usually starts with a 'Demand' or requirements - this could be for a physical part (inventory) or a service. A requisition is generated, which details the requirements (in some cases providing a requirements speciation) which actions the procurement department. An RFP or RFQ is then raised (request for proposal or Request for quotation.)

a. 1990 Clean Air Act
b. Purchasing process
c. Purchase requisition
d. Request for quotation

10. A _____ is a commercial document issued by a buyer to a seller, indicating types, quantities, and agreed prices for products or services the seller will provide to the buyer. Sending a _____ to a supplier constitutes a legal offer to buy products or services. Acceptance of a _____ by a seller usually forms a one-off contract between the buyer and seller, so no contract exists until the _____ is accepted.
a. 1990 Clean Air Act
b. Purchase order
c. 33 Strategies of War
d. 28-hour day

11. _____ is one of the managerial functions like planning, organizing, staffing and directing. It is an important function because it helps to check the errors and to take the corrective action so that deviation from standards are minimized and stated goals of the organization are achieved in desired manner.According to modern concepts, _____ is a foreseeing action whereas earlier concept of _____ was used only when errors were detected. _____ in management means setting standards, measuring actual performance and taking corrective action.

a. Decision tree pruning
b. Schedule of reinforcement
c. Control
d. Turnover

12. _____ is one of the four elements of marketing mix. An organization or set of organizations (go-betweens) involved in the process of making a product or service available for use or consumption by a consumer or business user.

The other three parts of the marketing mix are product, pricing, and promotion.

a. Matching theory
b. Distribution
c. Missing completely at random
d. Job creation programs

13. The _____ was a regulatory body in the United States created by the Interstate Commerce Act of 1887, which was signed into law by President Grover Cleveland. The agency was abolished in 1995, and the agency's remaining functions were transferred to the Surface Transportation Board.

The Commission's five members were appointed by the President with the consent of the United States Senate.

a. Extended Enterprise
b. American Institute of Industrial Engineers
c. United States Department of Agriculture
d. Interstate Commerce Commission

14. _____ is the provision of service to customers before, during and after a purchase.

According to Turban et al. (2002), '_____ is a series of activities designed to enhance the level of customer satisfaction - that is, the feeling that a product or service has met the customer expectation.'

Its importance varies by product, industry and customer; defective or broken merchandise can be exchanged, often only with a receipt and within a specified time frame.

Chapter 11. Supply Chain Management and E-Business

a. 28-hour day
b. 1990 Clean Air Act
c. Customer service
d. Service rate

15. _____ is an advertisement in which a particular product specifically mentions a competitor by name for the express purpose of showing why the competitor is inferior to the product naming it.

This should not be confused with parody advertisements, where a fictional product is being advertised for the purpose of poking fun at the particular advertisement, nor should it be confused with the use of a coined brand name for the purpose of comparing the product without actually naming an actual competitor. ('Wikipedia tastes better and is less filling than the Encyclopedia Galactica.')

In the 1980s, during what has been referred to as the cola wars, soft-drink manufacturer Pepsi ran a series of advertisements where people, caught on hidden camera, in a blind taste test, chose Pepsi over rival Coca-Cola.

a. 1990 Clean Air Act
b. 33 Strategies of War
c. 28-hour day
d. Comparative advertising

16. In mathematics, _____ is a technique for optimization of a linear objective function, subject to linear equality and linear inequality constraints. Informally, _____ determines the way to achieve the best outcome (such as maximum profit or lowest cost) in a given mathematical model and given some list of requirements represented as linear equations.

More formally, given a polytope (for example, a polygon or a polyhedron), and a real-valued affine function

$$f(x_1, x_2, \ldots, x_n) = c_1 x_1 + c_2 x_2 + \cdots + c_n x_n + d$$

defined on this polytope, a _____ method will find a point in the polytope where this function has the smallest (or largest) value.

a. Linear programming
b. 1990 Clean Air Act
c. Slack variable
d. Linear programming relaxation

Chapter 11. Supply Chain Management and E-Business

17. In economics, business, retail, and accounting, a _____ is the value of money that has been used up to produce something, and hence is not available for use anymore. In economics, a _____ is an alternative that is given up as a result of a decision. In business, the _____ may be one of acquisition, in which case the amount of money expended to acquire it is counted as _____.
    a. Cost overrun
    b. Fixed costs
    c. Cost allocation
    d. Cost

18. A _____ is a commercial building for storage of goods. _____s are used by manufacturers, importers, exporters, wholesalers, transport businesses, customs, etc. They are usually large plain buildings in industrial areas of cities and towns.
    a. 33 Strategies of War
    b. 28-hour day
    c. Warehouse
    d. 1990 Clean Air Act

19. _____ is a business term which refers to a range of software tools or modules used in executing supply chain transactions, managing supplier relationships and controlling associated business processes.

While functionality in such systems can often be broad - it commonly includes:

1. Customer requirement processing
2. Purchase order processing
3. Inventory management
4. Goods receipt and Warehouse management
5. Supplier Management/Sourcing

A requirement of many _____ often includes forecasting. Such tools often attempt to balance the disparity between supply and demand by improving business processes and using algorithms and consumption analysis to better plan future needs. _____ also often includes integration technology that allows organizations to trade electronically with supply chain partners.

   a. Demand chain
   b. Supply chain management software
   c. Supply-Chain Operations Reference
   d. Vendor Managed Inventory

Chapter 11. Supply Chain Management and E-Business

20. _____ is the process of comparing the cost, cycle time, productivity, or quality of a specific process or method to another that is widely considered to be an industry standard or best practice. Essentially, _____ provides a snapshot of the performance of your business and helps you understand where you are in relation to a particular standard. The result is often a business case for making changes in order to make improvements.

   a. Complementors
   b. Benchmarking
   c. Competitive heterogeneity
   d. Cost leadership

21. _____ is the branch of logistics that deals with the tangible components of a supply chain. Specifically, this covers the acquisition of spare parts and replacements, quality control of purchasing and ordering such parts, and the standards involved in ordering, shipping, and warehousing the said parts.

   A large component of _____ is ensuring that parts and materials used in the supply chain meet minimum requirements by performing quality assurance (QA.)

   a. Vendor Managed Inventory
   b. Supply-Chain Operations Reference
   c. Delayed differentiation
   d. Materials management

22. _____, commonly referred to as 'eBusiness' or 'e-Business', may be defined as the utilization of information and communication technologies (ICT) in support of all the activities of business. Commerce constitutes the exchange of products and services between businesses, groups and individuals and hence can be seen as one of the essential activities of any business. Hence, electronic commerce or eCommerce focuses on the use of ICT to enable the external activities and relationships of the business with individuals, groups and other businesses .

   a. A Stake in the Outcome
   b. A4e
   c. AAAI
   d. Electronic business

23. _____, commonly known as e-commerce, consists of the buying and selling of products or services over electronic systems such as the Internet and other computer networks. The amount of trade conducted electronically has grown extraordinarily with widespread Internet usage. The use of commerce is conducted in this way, spurring and drawing on innovations in electronic funds transfer, supply chain management, Internet marketing, online transaction processing, electronic data interchange (EDI), inventory management systems, and automated data collection systems.

a. A4e
b. A Stake in the Outcome
c. Electronic Commerce
d. Online shopping

24. _____ refers to the structured transmission of data between organizations by electronic means. It is used to transfer electronic documents from one computer system to another (ie) from one trading partner to another trading partner. It is more than mere E-mail; for instance, organizations might replace bills of lading and even checks with appropriate _____ messages.
   a. A Stake in the Outcome
   b. AAAI
   c. A4e
   d. Electronic Data Interchange

Chapter 12. Just-in-Time and Lean Manufacturing

1. _____ is an inventory strategy that strives to improve the return on investment of a business by reducing in-process inventory and its associated carrying costs. To meet _____ objectives, the process relies on signals between different points in the process. This means the process is often driven by a series of signals, or Kanban , which tell production when to make the next part. Kanban are usually 'tickets' but can be simple visual signals, such as the presence or absence of a part on a shelf. Implemented correctly, _____ can dramatically improve a manufacturing organization's return on investment, quality, and efficiency.
   a. Just-in-time
   b. 1990 Clean Air Act
   c. 28-hour day
   d. 33 Strategies of War

2. In probability theory, a probability distribution is called _____ if its cumulative distribution function is _____. This is equivalent to saying that for random variables X with the distribution in question, Pr[X = a] = 0 for all real numbers a, i.e.: the probability that X attains the value a is zero, for any number a. If the distribution of X is _____ then X is called a _____ random variable.
   a. Pay Band
   b. Decision tree pruning
   c. Connectionist expert systems
   d. Continuous

3. _____ or lean production, which is often known simply as 'Lean', is a production practice that considers the expenditure of resources for any goal other than the creation of value for the end customer to be wasteful, and thus a target for elimination. Working from the perspective of the customer who consumes a product or service, 'value' is defined as any action or process that a customer would be willing to pay for. Basically, lean is centered around creating more value with less work.
   a. Theory of constraints
   b. Six Sigma
   c. Lean manufacturing
   d. Production line

4. In queueing theory, _____ is the proportion of the system's resources which is used by the traffic which arrives at it. It should be strictly less than one for the system to function well. It is usually represented by the symbol ρ.
   a. Utilization
   b. A Stake in the Outcome
   c. AAAI
   d. A4e

Chapter 12. Just-in-Time and Lean Manufacturing

5. A time and motion study (or time-motion study) is a business efficiency technique combining the _____ work of Frederick Winslow Taylor with the Motion Study work of Frank and Lillian Gilbreth (not to be confused with their son, best known through the biographical 1950 film and book Cheaper by the Dozen.) It is a major part of scientific management (Taylorism.)

A time and motion study would be used to reduce the number of motions in performing a task in order to increase productivity.

   a. 33 Strategies of War
   b. 1990 Clean Air Act
   c. 28-hour day
   d. Time study

6. A _____ is the period of time between the initiation of any process of production and the completion of that process. Thus the _____ for ordering a new car from a manufacturer may be anywhere from 2 weeks to 6 months. In industry, _____ reduction is an important part of lean manufacturing.
   a. 33 Strategies of War
   b. 28-hour day
   c. 1990 Clean Air Act
   d. Lead time

7. _____ is an advertisement in which a particular product specifically mentions a competitor by name for the express purpose of showing why the competitor is inferior to the product naming it.

This should not be confused with parody advertisements, where a fictional product is being advertised for the purpose of poking fun at the particular advertisement, nor should it be confused with the use of a coined brand name for the purpose of comparing the product without actually naming an actual competitor. ('Wikipedia tastes better and is less filling than the Encyclopedia Galactica.')

In the 1980s, during what has been referred to as the cola wars, soft-drink manufacturer Pepsi ran a series of advertisements where people, caught on hidden camera, in a blind taste test, chose Pepsi over rival Coca-Cola.

   a. 33 Strategies of War
   b. 28-hour day
   c. Comparative advertising
   d. 1990 Clean Air Act

8. _____ is a management process whereby delivery (customer valued) processes are constantly evaluated and improved in the light of their efficiency, effectiveness and flexibility.

Some see it as a meta process for most management systems (Business Process Management, Quality Management, Project Management). Deming saw it as part of the 'system' whereby feedback from the process and customer were evaluated against organisational goals.

a. Sole proprietorship
b. First-mover advantage
c. Critical Success Factor
d. Continuous Improvement Process

9. _____ is a Japanese philosophy that focuses on continuous improvement throughout all aspects of life. When applied to the workplace, _____ activities continually improve all functions of a business, from manufacturing to management and from the CEO to the assembly line workers. By improving standardized activities and processes, _____ aims to eliminate waste .
a. Kaizen
b. Psychological pricing
c. Sensitivity analysis
d. Cross-docking

10. _____ is one of the many lean production methods for reducing waste in a manufacturing process. It provides a rapid and efficient way of converting a manufacturing process from running the current product to running the next product. This rapid changeover is key to reducing production lot sizes and thereby improving flow ' href='/wiki/Mura_'>Mura) The phrase 'single minute' does not mean that all changeovers and startups should take only one minute, but that they should take less than 10 minutes (in other words, 'single digit minute'.)
a. Statistical process control
b. Quality control
c. Process capability
d. Single Minute Exchange of Die

11. _____ refers to increasing the spiritual, political, social or economic strength of individuals and communities. It often involves the empowered developing confidence in their own capacities.

The term Human _____ covers a vast landscape of meanings, interpretations, definitions and disciplines ranging from psychology and philosophy to the highly commercialized Self-Help industry and Motivational sciences.

a. AAAI
b. A Stake in the Outcome
c. A4e
d. Empowerment

12. The _____ captures an expanded spectrum of values and criteria for measuring organizational success: economic, ecological and social. With the ratification of the United Nations and ICLEI _____ standard for urban and community accounting in early 2007, this became the dominant approach to public sector full cost accounting. Similar UN standards apply to natural capital and human capital measurement to assist in measurements required by _____, e.g. the ecoBudget standard for reporting ecological footprint.
   a. 33 Strategies of War
   b. 28-hour day
   c. 1990 Clean Air Act
   d. Triple bottom line

13. _____ is a concept related to lean and just-in-time (JIT) production. The Japanese word _____ is a common term meaning 'signboard' or 'billboard'. According to Taiichi Ohno, the man credited with developing JIT, _____ is a means through which JIT is achieved.
   a. Risk management
   b. Succession planning
   c. Trademark
   d. Kanban

14. _____s are a key component of Kanban, a signaling system common in Lean production, that utilizes cards to signal the need to move materials within a manufacturing or production facility or move materials from an outside supplier to the production facility.

The _____ is, in effect, a message that signals depletion of product, parts or inventory that when received will trigger the replenishment of that product, part or inventory. Consumption drives demand for more

   a. 33 Strategies of War
   b. 28-hour day
   c. 1990 Clean Air Act
   d. Kanban card

15. _____ is one of the managerial functions like planning, organizing, staffing and directing. It is an important function because it helps to check the errors and to take the corrective action so that deviation from standards are minimized and stated goals of the organization are achieved in desired manner. According to modern concepts, _____ is a foreseeing action whereas earlier concept of _____ was used only when errors were detected. _____ in management means setting standards, measuring actual performance and taking corrective action.

   a. Schedule of reinforcement
   b. Turnover
   c. Decision tree pruning
   d. Control

16. _____ is a Japanese term that means 'fail-safing' or 'mistake-proofing'. A _____ is any mechanism in a Lean manufacturing process that helps an equipment operator avoid (yokeru) mistakes (poka.) Its purpose is to eliminate product defects by preventing, correcting, or drawing attention to human errors as they occur.

   a. 28-hour day
   b. 1990 Clean Air Act
   c. 33 Strategies of War
   d. Poka-yoke

Chapter 13. Production Planning

1. _____ is an operational activity which does an aggregate plan for the production process, in advance of 2 to 18 months, to give an idea to management as to what quantity of materials and other resources are to be procured and when, so that the total cost of operations of the organization is kept to the minimum over that period.

The quantity of outsourcing, subcontracting of items, overtime of labor, numbers to be hired and fired in each period and the amount of inventory to be held in stock and to be backlogged for each period are decided. All of these activities are done within the framework of the company ethics, policies, and long term commitment to the society, community and the country of operation.

  a. A Stake in the Outcome
  b. Earned Schedule
  c. Earned value management
  d. Aggregate planning

2. _____ is one of the managerial functions like planning, organizing, staffing and directing. It is an important function because it helps to check the errors and to take the corrective action so that deviation from standards are minimized and stated goals of the organization are achieved in desired manner. According to modern concepts, _____ is a foreseeing action whereas earlier concept of _____ was used only when errors were detected. _____ in management means setting standards, measuring actual performance and taking corrective action.

  a. Decision tree pruning
  b. Schedule of reinforcement
  c. Turnover
  d. Control

3. In economics, _____ is the total demand for final goods and services in the economy (Y) at a given time and price level. It is the amount of goods and services in the economy that will be purchased at all possible price levels. This is the demand for the gross domestic product of a country when inventory levels are static.

  a. AAAI
  b. A Stake in the Outcome
  c. A4e
  d. Aggregate demand

4. In economics, _____ is the desire to own something and the ability to pay for it. The term _____ signifies the ability or the willingness to buy a particular commodity at a given point of time.

  a. 28-hour day
  b. 1990 Clean Air Act
  c. Demand
  d. 33 Strategies of War

5. _____ is the amount of time someone works beyond normal working hours. Normal hours may be determined in several ways:

- by custom (what is considered healthy or reasonable by society),
- by practices of a given trade or profession,
- by legislation,
- by agreement between employers and workers or their representatives.

Most nations have _____ laws designed to dissuade or prevent employers from forcing their employees to work excessively long hours. These laws may take into account other considerations than the humanitarian, such as increasing the overall level of employment in the economy. One common approach to regulating _____ is to require employers to pay workers at a higher hourly rate for _____ work.

 a. Organizational effectiveness
 b. Overtime
 c. Industrial relations
 d. Organizational structure

6. _____ is the temporary suspension or permanent termination of employment of an employee or (more commonly) a group of employees for business reasons, such as the decision that certain positions are no longer necessary or a business slow-down or interruption in work. Originally the term '_____' referred exclusively to a temporary interruption in work, as when factory work cyclically falls off. However, in recent times the term can also refer to the permanent elimination of a position.
 a. Termination of employment
 b. Wrongful dismissal
 c. Retirement
 d. Layoff

7. In economics, business, retail, and accounting, a _____ is the value of money that has been used up to produce something, and hence is not available for use anymore. In economics, a _____ is an alternative that is given up as a result of a decision. In business, the _____ may be one of acquisition, in which case the amount of money expended to acquire it is counted as _____.
 a. Cost
 b. Cost overrun
 c. Cost allocation
 d. Fixed costs

8. _____ is the process of determining the production capacity needed by an organization to meet changing demands for its products. In the context of _____, 'capacity' is the maximum amount of work that an organization is capable of completing in a given period of time.

A discrepancy between the capacity of an organization and the demands of its customers results in inefficiency, either in under-utilized resources or unfulfilled customers.

a. Remanufacturing
b. Scientific management
c. Productivity
d. Capacity planning

9. _____ is an advertisement in which a particular product specifically mentions a competitor by name for the express purpose of showing why the competitor is inferior to the product naming it.

This should not be confused with parody advertisements, where a fictional product is being advertised for the purpose of poking fun at the particular advertisement, nor should it be confused with the use of a coined brand name for the purpose of comparing the product without actually naming an actual competitor. ('Wikipedia tastes better and is less filling than the Encyclopedia Galactica.')

In the 1980s, during what has been referred to as the cola wars, soft-drink manufacturer Pepsi ran a series of advertisements where people, caught on hidden camera, in a blind taste test, chose Pepsi over rival Coca-Cola.

a. 28-hour day
b. 1990 Clean Air Act
c. 33 Strategies of War
d. Comparative advertising

10. _____ of the learning curve effect and the closely related experience curve effect express the relationship between equations for experience and efficiency or between efficiency gains and investment in the effort. The experience of 'learning curves' was first observed by the 19th Century German psychologist Hermann Ebbinghaus according to the difficulty of memorizing varying numbers of verbal stimuli, and subsequent learning about the complex processes of learning are discussed in the

The rule used for representing the learning curve effect states that the more times a task has been performed, the less time will be required on each subsequent iteration.

a. Spatial Decision Support Systems
b. Point biserial correlation coefficient
c. Distribution
d. Models

11. In mathematics, _____ is a technique for optimization of a linear objective function, subject to linear equality and linear inequality constraints. Informally, _____ determines the way to achieve the best outcome (such as maximum profit or lowest cost) in a given mathematical model and given some list of requirements represented as linear equations.

More formally, given a polytope (for example, a polygon or a polyhedron), and a real-valued affine function

$$f(x_1, x_2, \ldots, x_n) = c_1 x_1 + c_2 x_2 + \cdots + c_n x_n + d$$

defined on this polytope, a _____ method will find a point in the polytope where this function has the smallest (or largest) value.

a. Slack variable
b. 1990 Clean Air Act
c. Linear programming relaxation
d. Linear programming

12. In economics, _____' is the art or science of controlling economic demand to avoid a recession. In natural resources management and environmental policy more generally, it refers to policies to control consumer demand for environmentally sensitive or harmful goods such as water and energy. Within manufacturing firms the term is used to describe the activities of demand forecasting, planning and order fulfillment.
a. 33 Strategies of War
b. 1990 Clean Air Act
c. 28-hour day
d. Demand management

13. A _____ is a process in which a potential employee is evaluated by an employer for prospective employment in their company, organization and was established in the late 16th century.

A _____ typically precedes the hiring decision, and is used to evaluate the candidate. The interview is usually preceded by the evaluation of submitted résumés from interested candidates, then selecting a small number of candidates for interviews.

Chapter 13. Production Planning

a. Supported employment
b. Job interview
c. Payrolling
d. Split shift

14. A _____ is the period of time between the initiation of any process of production and the completion of that process. Thus the _____ for ordering a new car from a manufacturer may be anywhere from 2 weeks to 6 months. In industry, _____ reduction is an important part of lean manufacturing.
   a. Lead time
   b. 28-hour day
   c. 33 Strategies of War
   d. 1990 Clean Air Act

15. The _____ is the amount of time an organization will look into the future when preparing a strategic plan. Many commercial companies use a five-year _____, but other organizations such as the Forestry Commission in the UK have to use a much longer _____ to form effective plans.
   a. Psychological pricing
   b. Planning horizon
   c. Strategic Alliance
   d. No-bid contract

16. _____ is an inventory strategy that strives to improve the return on investment of a business by reducing in-process inventory and its associated carrying costs. To meet _____ objectives, the process relies on signals between different points in the process. This means the process is often driven by a series of signals, or Kanban, which tell production when to make the next part. Kanban are usually 'tickets' but can be simple visual signals, such as the presence or absence of a part on a shelf. Implemented correctly, _____ can dramatically improve a manufacturing organization's return on investment, quality, and efficiency.
   a. Just-in-time
   b. 33 Strategies of War
   c. 28-hour day
   d. 1990 Clean Air Act

17. _____ or lean production, which is often known simply as 'Lean', is a production practice that considers the expenditure of resources for any goal other than the creation of value for the end customer to be wasteful, and thus a target for elimination. Working from the perspective of the customer who consumes a product or service, 'value' is defined as any action or process that a customer would be willing to pay for. Basically, lean is centered around creating more value with less work.

a. Six Sigma
b. Lean manufacturing
c. Theory of constraints
d. Production line

18. _____ is a method of planning and managing projects that puts the main emphasis on the resources required to execute project tasks. It was developed by Eliyahu M. Goldratt. This is in contrast to the more traditional Critical Path and PERT methods, which emphasize task order and rigid scheduling. A Critical Chain project network will tend to keep the resources levelly loaded, but will require them to be flexible in their start times and to quickly switch between tasks and task chains to keep the whole project on schedule.
   a. Critical Chain Project Management
   b. Precedence diagram
   c. Project engineer
   d. Project management office

19. _____ is an overall management philosophy introduced by Dr. Eliyahu M. Goldratt in his 1984 book titled The Goal, that is geared to help organizations continually achieve their goal. The title comes from the contention that any manageable system is limited in achieving more of its goal by a very small number of constraints, and that there is always at least one constraint. The _____ process seeks to identify the constraint and restructure the rest of the organization around it, through the use of the Five Focusing Steps.
   a. Takt time
   b. Six Sigma
   c. Production line
   d. Theory of constraints

20. An _____, operating expenditure, operational expense, operational expenditure or OPEX is an on-going cost for running a product, business, or system. Its counterpart, a capital expenditure (CAPEX), is the cost of developing or providing non-consumable parts for the product or system. For example, the purchase of a photocopier is the CAPEX, and the annual paper and toner cost is the OPEX.
   a. AAAI
   b. A Stake in the Outcome
   c. Operating expense
   d. A4e

Chapter 14. Inventory Management

1. The phrase mergers and _____s refers to the aspect of corporate strategy, corporate finance and management dealing with the buying, selling and combining of different companies that can aid, finance, or help a growing company in a given industry grow rapidly without having to create another business entity.

An _____, also known as a takeover or a buyout, is the buying of one company (the 'target') by another. An _____ may be friendly or hostile.

   a. A4e
   b. A Stake in the Outcome
   c. Acquisition
   d. AAAI

2. In economics, business, retail, and accounting, a _____ is the value of money that has been used up to produce something, and hence is not available for use anymore. In economics, a _____ is an alternative that is given up as a result of a decision. In business, the _____ may be one of acquisition, in which case the amount of money expended to acquire it is counted as _____.
   a. Fixed costs
   b. Cost overrun
   c. Cost allocation
   d. Cost

3. In the fields of science, engineering, industry and statistics, _____ is the degree of closeness of a measured or calculated quantity to its actual (true) value. _____ is closely related to precision, also called reproducibility or repeatability, the degree to which further measurements or calculations show the same or similar results. _____ indicates proximity to the true value, precision to the repeatability or reproducibility of the measurement

The results of calculations or a measurement can be accurate but not precise, precise but not accurate, neither, or both.

   a. Accuracy
   b. AAAI
   c. A Stake in the Outcome
   d. A4e

4. The concept of _____ is a means to quantify the total cost of quality-related efforts and deficiencies. It was first described by Armand V. Feigenbaum in a 1956 Harvard Business Review article.

Prior to its introduction, the general perception was that higher quality requires higher costs, either by buying better materials or machines or by hiring more labor.

a. Cost overrun
b. Quality costs
c. Transaction cost
d. Variable cost

5. In economics, _____ is the desire to own something and the ability to pay for it. The term _____ signifies the ability or the willingness to buy a particular commodity at a given point of time.
   a. Demand
   b. 33 Strategies of War
   c. 1990 Clean Air Act
   d. 28-hour day

6. _____ is the level of inventory that minimizes the total inventory holding costs and ordering costs. The framework used to determine this order quantity is also known as Wilson _____ Model. The model was developed by F. W. Harris in 1913.
   a. Effective executive
   b. Event management
   c. Anti-leadership
   d. Economic order quantity

7. _____ is a financial mechanism in which a debtor obtains the right to delay payments to a creditor, for a defined period of time, in exchange for a charge or fee. Essentially, the party that owes money in the present purchases the right to delay the payment until some future date. The discount, or charge, is simply the difference between the original amount owed in the present and the amount that has to be paid in the future to settle the debt.
   a. Financial modeling
   b. Ruin theory
   c. Discounting
   d. Linear model

8. A _____ is the period of time between the initiation of any process of production and the completion of that process. Thus the _____ for ordering a new car from a manufacturer may be anywhere from 2 weeks to 6 months. In industry, _____ reduction is an important part of lean manufacturing.
   a. 28-hour day
   b. 1990 Clean Air Act
   c. 33 Strategies of War
   d. Lead time

Chapter 14. Inventory Management

9. In probability theory, a probability distribution is called _____ if its cumulative distribution function is _____. This is equivalent to saying that for random variables X with the distribution in question, Pr[X = a] = 0 for all real numbers a, i.e.: the probability that X attains the value a is zero, for any number a. If the distribution of X is _____ then X is called a _____ random variable.
   a. Pay Band
   b. Decision tree pruning
   c. Connectionist expert systems
   d. Continuous

10. In decision theory and estimation theory, the _____ of an estimator, $\hat{\theta}$, of an unknown parameter of the distribution, θ, is the expected value of the loss function

$$R(\theta, \hat{\theta}) = \mathbb{E}_\theta L(\theta, \hat{\theta}) = \int L(\theta, \hat{\theta})\, dP_\theta.$$

where dP_θ is a probability measure parametrized by θ.

- For a scalar parameter θ and a quadratic loss function,

$$L(\theta, \hat{\theta}) = (\theta - \hat{\theta})^2$$

   the _____ function becomes the mean squared error of the estimate,

$$R(\theta, \hat{\theta}) = E_\theta (\theta - \hat{\theta})^2$$

- In density estimation, the unknown parameter is probability density itself. The loss function is typically chosen to be a norm in an appropriate function space. For example, for L^2 norm,

$$L(f, \hat{f}) = \|f - \hat{f}\|_2^2$$

   the _____ function becomes the mean integrated squared error

$$R(f, \hat{f}) = E\|f - \hat{f}\|^2$$

Chapter 14. Inventory Management

a. Risk aversion
b. Linear model
c. Financial modeling
d. Risk

11. _____ is an advertisement in which a particular product specifically mentions a competitor by name for the express purpose of showing why the competitor is inferior to the product naming it.

This should not be confused with parody advertisements, where a fictional product is being advertised for the purpose of poking fun at the particular advertisement, nor should it be confused with the use of a coined brand name for the purpose of comparing the product without actually naming an actual competitor. ('Wikipedia tastes better and is less filling than the Encyclopedia Galactica.')

In the 1980s, during what has been referred to as the cola wars, soft-drink manufacturer Pepsi ran a series of advertisements where people, caught on hidden camera, in a blind taste test, chose Pepsi over rival Coca-Cola.

a. 33 Strategies of War
b. Comparative advertising
c. 28-hour day
d. 1990 Clean Air Act

12. _____ measures the performance of a system. Certain goals are defined and the _____ gives the percentage to which they should be achieved.

Examples

- Percentage of calls answered in a call center.
- Percentage of customers waiting less than a given fixed time.
- Percentage of customers that do not experience a stock out.

_____ is used in supply chain management and in inventory management to measure the performance of inventory systems.

Under stochastic conditions it is unavoidable that in some periods the inventory on hand is not sufficient to deliver the complete demand and, as a consequence, that part of the demand is filled only after an inventory-related waiting time.

a. Service level
b. 28-hour day
c. 33 Strategies of War
d. 1990 Clean Air Act

13. _____ is one of the four elements of marketing mix. An organization or set of organizations (go-betweens) involved in the process of making a product or service available for use or consumption by a consumer or business user.

The other three parts of the marketing mix are product, pricing, and promotion.

a. Distribution
b. Missing completely at random
c. Job creation programs
d. Matching theory

14. 'Speaking generally, properties are those physical quantities which directly describe the physical attributes of the system; _____s are those combinations of the properties which suffice to determine the response of the system. Properties can have all sorts of dimensions, depending upon the system being considered; _____s are dimensionless, or have the dimension of time or its reciprocal.'

The term can also be used in engineering contexts, however, as it is typically used in the physical sciences.

When the terms formal _____ and actual _____ are used, they generally correspond with the definitions used in computer science.

a. 33 Strategies of War
b. 1990 Clean Air Act
c. Parameter
d. 28-hour day

15. _____ is a term used by inventory specialists to describe a level of extra stock that is maintained below the cycle stock to buffer against stockouts. _____ exists to counter uncertainties in supply and demand. _____ is defined as extra units of inventory carried as protection against possible stockouts .(shortfall in raw material or packaging.)

a. Knowledge worker
b. Process automation
c. Safety stock
d. Product life cycle

16. _____ is a way of expressing knowledge or belief that an event will occur or has occurred. In mathematics the concept has been given an exact meaning in _____ theory, that is used extensively in such areas of study as mathematics, statistics, finance, gambling, science, and philosophy to draw conclusions about the likelihood of potential events and the underlying mechanics of complex systems.

The word _____ does not have a consistent direct definition.

a. Time series analysis
b. Standard deviation
c. Statistics
d. Probability

17. _____ of the learning curve effect and the closely related experience curve effect express the relationship between equations for experience and efficiency or between efficiency gains and investment in the effort. The experience of 'learning curves' was first observed by the 19th Century German psychologist Hermann Ebbinghaus according to the difficulty of memorizing varying numbers of verbal stimuli, and subsequent learning about the complex processes of learning are discussed in the

The rule used for representing the learning curve effect states that the more times a task has been performed, the less time will be required on each subsequent iteration.

a. Spatial Decision Support Systems
b. Models
c. Distribution
d. Point biserial correlation coefficient

18. _____ or economic opportunity loss is the value of the next best alternative forgone as the result of making a decision. _____ analysis is an important part of a company's decision-making processes but is not treated as an actual cost in any financial statement. The next best thing that a person can engage in is referred to as the _____ of doing the best thing and ignoring the next best thing to be done.

a. AAAI
b. A4e
c. A Stake in the Outcome
d. Opportunity cost

Chapter 14. Inventory Management

19. _____ is a family of business models in which the buyer of a product provides certain information to a supplier of that product and the supplier takes full responsibility for maintaining an agreed inventory of the material, usually at the buyer's consumption location (usually a store.) A third party logistics provider can also be involved to make sure that the buyer has the required level of inventory by adjusting the demand and supply gaps.

As a symbiotic relationship, _____ makes it less likely that a business will unintentionally become out of stock of a good and reduces inventory in the supply chain.

   a. Vendor Managed Inventory
   b. Supply Chain Risk Management
   c. Delayed differentiation
   d. Supply-Chain Operations Reference

Chapter 15. Resource Requirements Planning: MRP and CRP

1. _____ is a software based production planning and inventory control system used to manage manufacturing processes. Although it is not common nowadays, it is possible to conduct _____ by hand as well.

An _____ system is intended to simultaneously meet three objectives:

- Ensure materials and products are available for production and delivery to customers.
- Maintain the lowest possible level of inventory.
- Plan manufacturing activities, delivery schedules and purchasing activities.

Manufacturing organizations, whatever their products, face the same daily practical problem - that customers want products to be available in a shorter time than it takes to make them. This means that some level of planning is required.

a. 1990 Clean Air Act
b. 28-hour day
c. Material requirements planning
d. 33 Strategies of War

2. _____ is a list of the raw materials, sub-assemblies, intermediate assemblies, sub-components, components, parts and the quantities of each needed to manufacture an end item (final product) .
a. Piece rate
b. Bill of materials
c. Scientific management
d. Methods-time measurement

3. Government _____ are designed to show nonfinancial aspects of government operations. For example, a government financial report might include the number of arrests, number of convictions by crime category as well as the change (i.e., increase or decrease) in crime rate. Government _____ usually provide data on environmental conditions, education and conditions of streets and roads.
a. Privatization
b. Performance reports
c. 28-hour day
d. 1990 Clean Air Act

4. In economics, _____ is the desire to own something and the ability to pay for it. The term _____ signifies the ability or the willingness to buy a particular commodity at a given point of time.

Chapter 15. Resource Requirements Planning: MRP and CRP

   a. 28-hour day
   b. 33 Strategies of War
   c. 1990 Clean Air Act
   d. Demand

5. _____ is a term used by inventory specialists to describe a level of extra stock that is maintained below the cycle stock to buffer against stockouts. _____ exists to counter uncertainties in supply and demand. _____ is defined as extra units of inventory carried as protection against possible stockouts .(shortfall in raw material or packaging.)

   a. Process automation
   b. Product life cycle
   c. Knowledge worker
   d. Safety stock

6. A _____ is a process in which a potential employee is evaluated by an employer for prospective employment in their company, organization and was established in the late 16th century.

A _____ typically precedes the hiring decision, and is used to evaluate the candidate. The interview is usually preceded by the evaluation of submitted résumés from interested candidates, then selecting a small number of candidates for interviews.

   a. Split shift
   b. Job interview
   c. Supported employment
   d. Payrolling

7. _____ is a company-wide computer software system used to manage and coordinate all the resources, information, and functions of a business from shared data stores.

An _____ system has a service-oriented architecture with modular hardware and software units and 'services' that communicate on a local area network. The modular design allows a business to add or reconfigure modules (perhaps from different vendors) while preserving data integrity in one shared database that may be centralized or distributed.

   a. A4e
   b. A Stake in the Outcome
   c. AAAI
   d. Enterprise resource planning

Chapter 15. Resource Requirements Planning: MRP and CRP

8. _____ is defined by APICS as a method for the effective planning of all resources of a manufacturing company. Ideally, it addresses operational planning in units, financial planning in dollars, and has a simulation capability to answer 'what-if' questions and extension of closed-loop _____. Manufacturing resource planning (or Manufacturing resource planning2) - Around 1980, over-frequent changes in sales forecasts, entailing continual readjustments in production, as well as the unsuitability of the parameters fixed by the system, led _____ (Material Requirement Planning) to evolve into a new concept : _____ (e.g. _____ 2)

This is not exclusively a software function, but a marriage of people skills, dedication to data base accuracy, and computer resources.

   a. MRP II
   b. Jidoka
   c. Manufacturing resource planning
   d. Homeworkers

9. A _____ is a computer program typically used to provide some form of artificial intelligence, which consists primarily of a set of rules about behavior. These rules, termed productions, are a basic representation found useful in AI planning, expert systems and action selection. A _____ provides the mechanism necessary to execute productions in order to achieve some goal for the system.
   a. 33 Strategies of War
   b. Production system
   c. 1990 Clean Air Act
   d. 28-hour day

10. A _____ is the period of time between the initiation of any process of production and the completion of that process. Thus the _____ for ordering a new car from a manufacturer may be anywhere from 2 weeks to 6 months. In industry, _____ reduction is an important part of lean manufacturing.
   a. 28-hour day
   b. 1990 Clean Air Act
   c. Lead time
   d. 33 Strategies of War

Chapter 16. Manufacturing Operations Scheduling

1. _____ are typically small manufacturing operations that handle specialized manufacturing processes such as small customer orders or small batch jobs. _____ typically move on to different jobs (possibly with different customers) when each job is completed. By nature of this type of manufacturing operation, _____ are usually specialized in skill and processes.
    a. 1990 Clean Air Act
    b. 33 Strategies of War
    c. Job shops
    d. 28-hour day

2. _____ is one of the managerial functions like planning, organizing, staffing and directing. It is an important function because it helps to check the errors and to take the corrective action so that deviation from standards are minimized and stated goals of the organization are achieved in desired manner. According to modern concepts, _____ is a foreseeing action whereas earlier concept of _____ was used only when errors were detected. _____ in management means setting standards, measuring actual performance and taking corrective action.
    a. Schedule of reinforcement
    b. Decision tree pruning
    c. Turnover
    d. Control

3. A _____ is a type of bar chart that illustrates a project schedule. _____s illustrate the start and finish dates of the terminal elements and summary elements of a project. Terminal elements and summary elements comprise the work breakdown structure of the project.
    a. 1990 Clean Air Act
    b. 28-hour day
    c. 33 Strategies of War
    d. Gantt chart

4. In economics, business, retail, and accounting, a _____ is the value of money that has been used up to produce something, and hence is not available for use anymore. In economics, a _____ is an alternative that is given up as a result of a decision. In business, the _____ may be one of acquisition, in which case the amount of money expended to acquire it is counted as _____.
    a. Cost allocation
    b. Cost overrun
    c. Fixed costs
    d. Cost

5. In mathematics, _____ is a technique for optimization of a linear objective function, subject to linear equality and linear inequality constraints. Informally, _____ determines the way to achieve the best outcome (such as maximum profit or lowest cost) in a given mathematical model and given some list of requirements represented as linear equations.

More formally, given a polytope (for example, a polygon or a polyhedron), and a real-valued affine function

$$f(x_1, x_2, \ldots, x_n) = c_1 x_1 + c_2 x_2 + \cdots + c_n x_n + d$$

defined on this polytope, a _____ method will find a point in the polytope where this function has the smallest (or largest) value.

a. Linear programming
b. 1990 Clean Air Act
c. Slack variable
d. Linear programming relaxation

6. The _____ is one of the fundamental combinatorial optimization problems in the branch of optimization or operations research in mathematics. It consists of finding a maximum weight matching in a weighted bipartite graph.

In its most general form, the problem is as follows:

There are a number of agents and a number of tasks.

a. A4e
b. A Stake in the Outcome
c. AAAI
d. Assignment problem

7. In probability theory, a probability distribution is called _____ if its cumulative distribution function is _____. This is equivalent to saying that for random variables X with the distribution in question, Pr[X = a] = 0 for all real numbers a, i.e.: the probability that X attains the value a is zero, for any number a. If the distribution of X is _____ then X is called a _____ random variable.

a. Connectionist expert systems
b. Pay Band
c. Continuous
d. Decision tree pruning

8. A _____ is an enterprise software application that is in charge of unattended background executions, commonly known for historical reasons as batch processing.

Synonyms are batch system, Distributed Resource Management System (DRMS), and Distributed Resource Manager (DRM.) Today's _____s typically provide a graphical user interface and a single point of control for definition and monitoring of background executions in a distributed network of computers.

   a. 33 Strategies of War
   b. 1990 Clean Air Act
   c. 28-hour day
   d. Job scheduler

9. _____ is an overall management philosophy introduced by Dr. Eliyahu M. Goldratt in his 1984 book titled The Goal, that is geared to help organizations continually achieve their goal. The title comes from the contention that any manageable system is limited in achieving more of its goal by a very small number of constraints, and that there is always at least one constraint. The _____ process seeks to identify the constraint and restructure the rest of the organization around it, through the use of the Five Focusing Steps.

   a. Theory of constraints
   b. Production line
   c. Six Sigma
   d. Takt time

Chapter 17. Quality Control

1. In engineering and manufacturing, _____ and quality engineering are used in developing systems to ensure products or services are designed and produced to meet or exceed customer requirements. Refer to the definition by Merriam-Webster for further information . These systems are often developed in conjunction with other business and engineering disciplines using a cross-functional approach.
    a. Statistical process control
    b. Single Minute Exchange of Die
    c. Process capability
    d. Quality control

2. _____ is one of the managerial functions like planning, organizing, staffing and directing. It is an important function because it helps to check the errors and to take the corrective action so that deviation from standards are minimized and stated goals of the organization are achieved in desired manner.According to modern concepts, _____ is a foreseeing action whereas earlier concept of _____ was used only when errors were detected. _____ in management means setting standards, measuring actual performance and taking corrective action.
    a. Schedule of reinforcement
    b. Turnover
    c. Control
    d. Decision tree pruning

3. A _____ is a computer program typically used to provide some form of artificial intelligence, which consists primarily of a set of rules about behavior. These rules, termed productions, are a basic representation found useful in AI planning, expert systems and action selection. A _____ provides the mechanism necessary to execute productions in order to achieve some goal for the system.
    a. 33 Strategies of War
    b. Production system
    c. 1990 Clean Air Act
    d. 28-hour day

4. _____ is an advertisement in which a particular product specifically mentions a competitor by name for the express purpose of showing why the competitor is inferior to the product naming it.

This should not be confused with parody advertisements, where a fictional product is being advertised for the purpose of poking fun at the particular advertisement, nor should it be confused with the use of a coined brand name for the purpose of comparing the product without actually naming an actual competitor. ('Wikipedia tastes better and is less filling than the Encyclopedia Galactica.')

In the 1980s, during what has been referred to as the cola wars, soft-drink manufacturer Pepsi ran a series of advertisements where people, caught on hidden camera, in a blind taste test, chose Pepsi over rival Coca-Cola.

a. 28-hour day
b. 33 Strategies of War
c. 1990 Clean Air Act
d. Comparative advertising

5. A sample is a subject chosen from a population for investigation. A _____ is one chosen by a method involving an unpredictable component. Random sampling can also refer to taking a number of independent observations from the same probability distribution, without involving any real population.
   a. Random sample
   b. 1990 Clean Air Act
   c. 28-hour day
   d. 33 Strategies of War

6. In probability theory, the _____ states conditions under which the sum of a sufficiently large number of independent random variables, each with finite mean and variance, will be approximately normally distributed. Since real-world quantities are often the balanced sum of many unobserved random events, this theorem provides a partial explanation for the prevalence of the normal probability distribution. The _____ also justifies the approximation of large-sample statistics to the normal distribution in controlled experiments.
   a. Point biserial correlation coefficient
   b. Pay Band
   c. Heavy-tailed distributions
   d. Central limit theorem

7. The _____ in statistical process control is a tool used to determine whether a manufacturing or business process is in a state of statistical control or not.

If the chart indicates that the process is currently under control then it can be used with confidence to predict the future performance of the process. If the chart indicates that the process being monitored is not in control, the pattern it reveals can help determine the source of variation to be eliminated to bring the process back into control.

   a. Control chart
   b. Time series analysis
   c. Simple moving average
   d. Failure rate

8. _____ is one of the four elements of marketing mix. An organization or set of organizations (go-betweens) involved in the process of making a product or service available for use or consumption by a consumer or business user.

The other three parts of the marketing mix are product, pricing, and promotion.

a. Distribution
b. Missing completely at random
c. Job creation programs
d. Matching theory

9. _____ is an effective method of monitoring a process through the use of control charts. Control charts enable the use of objective criteria for distinguishing background variation from events of significance based on statistical techniques. Much of its power lies in the ability to monitor both process center and its variation about that center.
a. Single Minute Exchange of Die
b. Quality control
c. Process capability
d. Statistical process control

10. In decision theory and estimation theory, the _____ of an estimator, $\hat{\theta}$, of an unknown parameter of the distribution, θ, is the expected value of the loss function

$$R(\theta, \hat{\theta}) = \mathbb{E}_\theta L(\theta, \hat{\theta}) = \int L(\theta, \hat{\theta}) \, dP_\theta.$$

where dP_θ is a probability measure parametrized by θ.

- For a scalar parameter θ and a quadratic loss function,

$$L(\theta, \hat{\theta}) = (\theta - \hat{\theta})^2$$

the _____ function becomes the mean squared error of the estimate,

$$R(\theta, \hat{\theta}) = E_\theta (\theta - \hat{\theta})^2$$

- In density estimation, the unknown parameter is probability density itself. The loss function is typically chosen to be a norm in an appropriate function space. For example, for L^2 norm,

$$L(f, \hat{f}) = \|f - \hat{f}\|_2^2$$

the _____ function becomes the mean integrated squared error

$$R(f, \hat{f}) = E\|f - \hat{f}\|^2$$

a. Risk aversion
b. Financial modeling
c. Linear model
d. Risk

11. Engineering _____ is the permissible limit of variation in

   1. a physical dimension,
   2. a measured value or physical property of a material, manufactured object, system, or service,
   3. other measured values (such as temperature, humidity, etc.)
   4. in engineering and safety, a physical distance or space (_____), as in a truck (lorry), train or boat under a bridge as well as a train in a tunnel

Dimensions, properties, or conditions may vary within certain practical limits without significantly affecting functioning of equipment or a process. _____s are specified to allow reasonable leeway for imperfections and inherent variability without compromising performance.

The _____ may be specified as a factor or percentage of the nominal value, a maximum deviation from a nominal value, an explicit range of allowed values, be specified by a note or published standard with this information, or be implied by the numeric accuracy of the nominal value. _____ can be symmetrical, as in 40±0.1, or asymmetrical, such as 40+0.2/−0.1.

a. Zero defects
b. Quality assurance
c. Root cause analysis
d. Tolerance

12. A _____ is a type of bar chart that illustrates a project schedule. _____s illustrate the start and finish dates of the terminal elements and summary elements of a project. Terminal elements and summary elements comprise the work breakdown structure of the project.
a. 28-hour day
b. 33 Strategies of War
c. 1990 Clean Air Act
d. Gantt chart

13. _____ refers to the movement of cash into or out of a business or financial product. It is usually measured during a specified, finite period of time. Measurement of _____ can be used

- to determine a project's rate of return or value. The time of _____s into and out of projects are used as inputs in financial models such as internal rate of return, and net present value.
- to determine problems with a business's liquidity. Being profitable does not necessarily mean being liquid. A company can fail because of a shortage of cash, even while profitable.
- as an alternate measure of a business's profits when it is believed that accrual accounting concepts do not represent economic realities. For example, a company may be notionally profitable but generating little operational cash (as may be the case for a company that barters its products rather than selling for cash.) In such a case, the company may be deriving additional operating cash by issuing shares evaluating default risk, re-investment requirements, etc.

_____ is a generic term used differently depending on the context. It may be defined by users for their own purposes.

a. Gross profit
b. Gross profit margin
c. Sweat equity
d. Cash flow

14. _____ is a mathematical science pertaining to the collection, analysis, interpretation or explanation, and presentation of data. It also provides tools for prediction and forecasting based on data. It is applicable to a wide variety of academic disciplines, from the natural and social sciences to the humanities, government and business.
   a. Simple moving average
   b. Failure rate
   c. Location parameter
   d. Statistics

Chapter 18. Employee Productivity

1. _____ refers to metrics and measures of output from production processes, per unit of input. Labor _____, for example, is typically measured as a ratio of output per labor-hour, an input. _____ may be conceived of as a metrics of the technical or engineering efficiency of production.
    a. Remanufacturing
    b. Master production schedule
    c. Value engineering
    d. Productivity

2. _____ is a mathematical science pertaining to the collection, analysis, interpretation or explanation, and presentation of data. It also provides tools for prediction and forecasting based on data. It is applicable to a wide variety of academic disciplines, from the natural and social sciences to the humanities, government and business.
    a. Failure rate
    b. Location parameter
    c. Simple moving average
    d. Statistics

3. The _____ or gross domestic income (GDI), a basic measure of an economy's economic performance, is the market value of all final goods and services made within the borders of a nation in a year. _____ can be defined in three ways, all of which are conceptually identical. First, it is equal to the total expenditures for all final goods and services produced within the country in a stipulated period of time (usually a 365-day year).
    a. Perfect competition
    b. Productivity management
    c. Human capital
    d. Gross domestic product

4. _____ is the amount of goods and services that a labourer produces in a given amount of time. It is one of several types of productivity that economists measure. _____ can be measured for a firm, a process or a country.
    a. Business Network Transformation
    b. Labour productivity
    c. Time and attendance
    d. Retroactive overtime

5. _____ refers to training in different ways to improve overall performance. It takes advantage of the particular effectiveness of each training method, while at the same time attempting to neglect the shortcomings of that method by combining it with other methods that address its weaknesses.

Cross training is employee-employer field means, training employees to do one another's work.

a. Cross-training
b. 28-hour day
c. 1990 Clean Air Act
d. 33 Strategies of War

6. _____ means increasing the scope of a job through extending the range of its job duties and responsibilities. This contradicts the principles of specialisation and the division of labour whereby work is divided into small units, each of which is performed repetitively by an individual worker. Some motivational theories suggest that the boredom and alienation caused by the division of labour can actually cause efficiency to fall.

   a. Mock interview
   b. Job enlargement
   c. Delayering
   d. Centralization

7. _____ is an attempt to motivate employees by giving them the opportunity to use the range of their abilities. It is an idea that was developed by the American psychologist Frederick Herzberg in the 1950s. It can be contrasted to job enlargement which simply increases the number of tasks without changing the challenge.

   a. Cash cow
   b. C-A-K-E
   c. Job enrichment
   d. Catfish effect

8. _____ refers to increasing the spiritual, political, social or economic strength of individuals and communities. It often involves the empowered developing confidence in their own capacities.

The term Human _____ covers a vast landscape of meanings, interpretations, definitions and disciplines ranging from psychology and philosophy to the highly commercialized Self-Help industry and Motivational sciences.

   a. Empowerment
   b. AAAI
   c. A Stake in the Outcome
   d. A4e

9. _____ is the state or fact of exclusive rights and control over property, which may be an object, land/real estate or intellectual property. An _____ right is also referred to as title. The concept of _____ has existed for thousands of years and in all cultures.

a. Emanation of the state
b. A Stake in the Outcome
c. A4e
d. Ownership

10. _____ are conventions, treaties and recommendations designed to eliminate unjust and inhumane labour practices. The primary inernational agency charged with developing such standards is the International Labour Organization (ILO.) Established in 1919, the ILO advocates international standards as essential for the eradication of labour conditions involving 'injustice, hardship and privation'.

a. Airbus Industrie
b. Airbus SAS
c. International labour standards
d. Anaconda Copper

11. In statistics, _____ is:

- the arithmetic _____
- the expected value of a random variable, which is also called the population _____.

It is sometimes stated that the '_____' _____s average. This is incorrect if '_____' is taken in the specific sense of 'arithmetic _____' as there are different types of averages: the _____, median, and mode. Other simple statistical analyses use measures of spread, such as range, interquartile range, or standard deviation. For a real-valued random variable X, the _____ is the expectation of X. Note that not every probability distribution has a defined _____; see the Cauchy distribution for an example.

a. Statistical inference
b. Control chart
c. Correlation
d. Mean

12. The _____ system was developed by AMD in the mid-1990s as a method of comparing their x86 processors to those of rival Intel.

The first use of the _____ system was in 1996, when AMD used it to assert that their AMD 5x86 processor was as fast as a Pentium running at 75 MHz. The designation 'P75' was added to the chip to denote this.

Chapter 18. Employee Productivity

a. Performance rating
b. 1990 Clean Air Act
c. 33 Strategies of War
d. 28-hour day

13. A time and motion study (or time-motion study) is a business efficiency technique combining the _____ work of Frederick Winslow Taylor with the Motion Study work of Frank and Lillian Gilbreth (not to be confused with their son, best known through the biographical 1950 film and book Cheaper by the Dozen.) It is a major part of scientific management (Taylorism.)

A time and motion study would be used to reduce the number of motions in performing a task in order to increase productivity.

a. Time study
b. 33 Strategies of War
c. 1990 Clean Air Act
d. 28-hour day

14. The term _____ refers to a graphical representation of the 'average' rate of learning for an activity or tool. It can represent at a glance the initial difficulty of learning something and, to an extent, how much there is to learn after initial familiarity. For example, the Windows program Notepad is extremely simple to learn, but offers little after this.
a. 33 Strategies of War
b. 1990 Clean Air Act
c. 28-hour day
d. Learning curve

Chapter 19. Maintenance Management

1. _____, a business term, is a measure of how products and services supplied by a company meet or surpass customer expectation. It is seen as a key performance indicator within business and is part of the four perspectives of a Balanced Scorecard.

In a competitive marketplace where businesses compete for customers, _____ is seen as a key differentiator and increasingly has become a key element of business strategy.

   a. Foreign ownership
   b. Horizontal integration
   c. Critical Success Factor
   d. Customer satisfaction

2. In economics, the _____ is the theory that the price of an object or condition is determined by the sum of the cost of the resources that went into making it. The cost can compose any of the factors of production (including labour, capital, or land) and taxation.

The theory makes the most sense under assumptions of constant returns to scale and the existence of just one non-produced factor of production.

   a. 28-hour day
   b. 1990 Clean Air Act
   c. 33 Strategies of War
   d. Cost-of-production theory of value

3. In economics, business, retail, and accounting, a _____ is the value of money that has been used up to produce something, and hence is not available for use anymore. In economics, a _____ is an alternative that is given up as a result of a decision. In business, the _____ may be one of acquisition, in which case the amount of money expended to acquire it is counted as _____.
   a. Cost allocation
   b. Cost overrun
   c. Fixed costs
   d. Cost

4. _____ has the following meanings:

Chapter 19. Maintenance Management

The care and servicing by personnel for the purpose of maintaining equipment and facilities in satisfactory operating condition by providing for systematic inspection, detection, and correction of incipient failures either before they occur or before they develop into major defects.

1. Maintenance, including tests, measurements, adjustments, and parts replacement, performed specifically to prevent faults from occurring.

While _____ is generally considered to be worthwhile, there are risks such as equipment failure or human error involved when performing _____, just as in any maintenance operation. _____ as scheduled overhaul or scheduled replacement provides two of the three proactive failure management policies available to the maintenance engineer. Common methods of determining what _____ failure management policies should be applied are; OEM recommendations, requirements of codes and legislation within a jurisdiction, what an 'expert' thinks ought to be done, or the maintenance that's already done to similar equipment.

   a. 28-hour day
   b. Preventive maintenance
   c. 1990 Clean Air Act
   d. 33 Strategies of War

5. _____ is an advertisement in which a particular product specifically mentions a competitor by name for the express purpose of showing why the competitor is inferior to the product naming it.

This should not be confused with parody advertisements, where a fictional product is being advertised for the purpose of poking fun at the particular advertisement, nor should it be confused with the use of a coined brand name for the purpose of comparing the product without actually naming an actual competitor. ('Wikipedia tastes better and is less filling than the Encyclopedia Galactica.')

In the 1980s, during what has been referred to as the cola wars, soft-drink manufacturer Pepsi ran a series of advertisements where people, caught on hidden camera, in a blind taste test, chose Pepsi over rival Coca-Cola.

   a. 33 Strategies of War
   b. 1990 Clean Air Act
   c. Comparative advertising
   d. 28-hour day

6. _____ is fixing any sort of mechanical or electrical device should it become out of order or broken (known as repair, unscheduled or casualty maintenance) as well as performing the routine actions which keep the device in working order (known as scheduled maintenance) or prevent trouble from arising (preventive maintenance.) MRO may be defined as, 'All actions which have the objective of retaining or restoring an item in or to a state in which it can perform its required function. The actions include the combination of all technical and corresponding administrative, managerial, and supervision actions.'

Chapter 19. Maintenance Management 115

MRO operations can be categorised by whether the product remains the property of the customer, i.e., a service is being offer or whether the product is brought by the reprocessing organisation and sold to any customer wishing to make the purchase.

   a. 33 Strategies of War
   b. 1990 Clean Air Act
   c. 28-hour day
   d. Maintenance, repair and operations

7. A _____ is a change implemented to address a weakness identified in a management system. Normally _____s are implemented in response to a customer complaint, abnormal levels of internal nonconformity, nonconformities identified during an internal audit or adverse or unstable trends in product and process monitoring such as would be identified by SPC.

The process of determining a _____ requires identification of actions that can be taken to prevent or mitigate the weakness.

   a. 1990 Clean Air Act
   b. 28-hour day
   c. Corrective action
   d. Zero defects

8. _____ is the use of control systems (such as numerical control, programmable logic control, and other industrial control systems), in concert with other applications of information technology (such as computer-aided technologies [CAD, CAM, CAx]), to control industrial machinery and processes, reducing the need for human intervention. In the scope of industrialization, _____ is a step beyond mechanization. Whereas mechanization provided human operators with machinery to assist them with the physical requirements of work, _____ greatly reduces the need for human sensory and mental requirements as well.
   a. AAAI
   b. Automation
   c. A Stake in the Outcome
   d. A4e

9. The _____ is given by the United States National Institute of Standards and Technology. Through the actions of the National Productivity Advisory Committee chaired by Jack Grayson, it was established by the Malcolm Baldrige National Quality Improvement Act of 1987 - Public Law 100-107 and named for Malcolm Baldrige, who served as United States Secretary of Commerce during the Reagan administration from 1981 until his 1987 death in a rodeo accident. APQC, , organized the first White House Conference on Productivity, spearheading the creation and design of the _____ in 1987, and jointly administering the award for its first three years.

a. Scenario planning
b. Malcolm Baldrige National Quality Award
c. Business Network Transformation
d. Time and attendance

10. _____ refers to the movement of cash into or out of a business or financial product. It is usually measured during a specified, finite period of time. Measurement of _____ can be used

- to determine a project's rate of return or value. The time of _____s into and out of projects are used as inputs in financial models such as internal rate of return, and net present value.
- to determine problems with a business's liquidity. Being profitable does not necessarily mean being liquid. A company can fail because of a shortage of cash, even while profitable.
- as an alternate measure of a business's profits when it is believed that accrual accounting concepts do not represent economic realities. For example, a company may be notionally profitable but generating little operational cash (as may be the case for a company that barters its products rather than selling for cash.) In such a case, the company may be deriving additional operating cash by issuing shares evaluating default risk, re-investment requirements, etc.

_____ is a generic term used differently depending on the context. It may be defined by users for their own purposes.

a. Sweat equity
b. Cash flow
c. Gross profit margin
d. Gross profit

11. The term '_____' refers to the concept of collecting information and attempting to spot a pattern in the information. In some fields of study, the term '_____' has more formally-defined meanings.

In project management _____ is a mathematical technique that uses historical results to predict future outcome.

a. Regression analysis
b. Least squares
c. Stepwise regression
d. Trend analysis

12. In mathematical logic, _____ is a valid argument and rule of inference which makes the inference that, if the conjunction A and B is true, then A is true, and B is true.

In formal language:

$$A \wedge B \vdash A$$

or

$$A \wedge B \vdash B$$

The argument has one premise, namely a conjunction, and one often uses _____ in longer arguments to derive one of the conjuncts.

An example in English:

>It's raining and it's pouring.

a. 1990 Clean Air Act
b. Fuzzy logic
c. Validity
d. Simplification

Chapter 1
1. c 2. b 3. d 4. c 5. d 6. d 7. d 8. c 9. d 10. c
11. d 12. d 13. d 14. d 15. b 16. d 17. d 18. b 19. c

Chapter 2
1. b 2. a 3. c 4. d 5. c 6. d 7. d 8. b 9. b 10. d
11. a 12. c 13. a 14. d 15. b 16. d 17. d 18. d 19. b 20. d
21. a 22. d 23. a 24. b

Chapter 3
1. d 2. c 3. a 4. d 5. d 6. b 7. b 8. d 9. a 10. d
11. b 12. a 13. b 14. a 15. d 16. d 17. b 18. a 19. d 20. a
21. a 22. d 23. b 24. a 25. b 26. d 27. b 28. d 29. b 30. c
31. d 32. d 33. d 34. a 35. b

Chapter 4
1. c 2. d 3. d 4. d 5. c 6. c 7. d 8. d 9. d 10. d
11. c 12. b 13. b 14. d 15. d 16. a 17. b 18. d 19. d 20. b
21. d 22. d 23. b 24. d 25. d 26. d 27. a 28. c 29. d 30. b
31. a 32. c

Chapter 5
1. d 2. d 3. d 4. d 5. d 6. d 7. d 8. c 9. c 10. d
11. d 12. a 13. d 14. b 15. a 16. b 17. b 18. d 19. d 20. d
21. b 22. c 23. a 24. b 25. d

Chapter 6
1. b 2. b 3. c 4. d 5. b 6. b 7. d 8. c 9. c 10. d
11. d 12. d 13. d 14. b 15. a 16. d 17. b 18. b 19. d

Chapter 7
1. d 2. d 3. d 4. a 5. b 6. a 7. d 8. d 9. a 10. c
11. d 12. c 13. c 14. a 15. a 16. b 17. b 18. d 19. d 20. b
21. d 22. d 23. a 24. d 25. b 26. d 27. d 28. d 29. d 30. b
31. a

Chapter 8
1. d 2. b 3. d 4. b 5. c 6. d 7. d 8. d

Chapter 9
1. d 2. c 3. d 4. c 5. a 6. d

Chapter 10
1. a 2. c 3. c 4. c 5. d 6. b 7. c 8. b 9. c 10. d
11. d 12. d 13. d 14. b 15. c 16. d

ANSWER KEY

Chapter 11
1. c	2. d	3. d	4. c	5. a	6. d	7. d	8. a	9. b	10. b
11. c	12. b	13. d	14. c	15. d	16. a	17. d	18. c	19. b	20. b
21. d	22. d	23. c	24. d						

Chapter 12
1. a	2. d	3. c	4. a	5. d	6. d	7. c	8. d	9. a	10. d
11. d	12. d	13. d	14. d	15. d	16. d				

Chapter 13
1. d	2. d	3. d	4. c	5. b	6. d	7. a	8. d	9. d	10. d
11. d	12. d	13. b	14. a	15. b	16. a	17. b	18. a	19. d	20. c

Chapter 14
1. c	2. d	3. a	4. b	5. a	6. d	7. c	8. d	9. d	10. d
11. b	12. a	13. a	14. c	15. c	16. d	17. b	18. d	19. a	

Chapter 15
1. c	2. b	3. b	4. d	5. d	6. b	7. d	8. c	9. b	10. c

Chapter 16
1. c	2. d	3. d	4. d	5. a	6. d	7. c	8. d	9. a

Chapter 17
1. d	2. c	3. b	4. d	5. a	6. d	7. a	8. a	9. d	10. d
11. d	12. d	13. d	14. d						

Chapter 18
1. d	2. d	3. d	4. b	5. a	6. b	7. c	8. a	9. d	10. c
11. d	12. a	13. a	14. d						

Chapter 19
1. d	2. d	3. d	4. b	5. c	6. d	7. c	8. b	9. b	10. b
11. d	12. d								

www.ingramcontent.com/pod-product-compliance
Lightning Source LLC
Chambersburg PA
CBHW082049230426
43670CB00016B/2826